Vases of the Sea

VASES OF THE SEA

FAR EASTERN PORCELAIN
AND OTHER TREASURES

Felicia Schuster and Cecilia Wolseley

Charles Scribner's Sons
New York

Photographs by Donald Southern
Design by Colin Reed

Printed in Great Britain
Library of Congress Catalog Card Number 73–7215
SBN 684–13556–6 (cloth)

To Nona and Horace Renshaw,
without whose help and encouragement
this book would never have been written,
and to Blanche, in grateful thanks

Contents

China

China and Japan

Japan

Appendix

Foreword

The authors have asked me to write a few words to introduce this book on behalf of my late partner, Mr Stanley Hutson, who unfortunately died while it was being written. Mr Hutson had studied oriental ceramics, with Cecilia Wolseley's help, for a few years only, but nevertheless he had the honour to be made a member of the *Oriental Ceramic Society* shortly before his death. He became an enthusiastic collector of oriental pottery and porcelain, and some of his pieces are introduced in this book. He also gave the authors much valuable advice in their work, proving that an amateur who studies merely for the sheer joy of it may find himself in the inner circle of professionals.

MURIEL TAYLOR

London

Preface

Whilst looking round sale-rooms and junk-shops we were impressed by the endless variety of Chinese and Japanese ceramics, standing out strikingly among the other objects. A quotation from Addison seems almost as apt today as it was when written in *The Lounger* in 1786: 'In the ornamental porcelain the eye was completely lost in a chaos of pagodas – wagging-headed mandarins, red lions, golden dogs and fiery dragons.' The eye does indeed seem to be lost in chaos when it comes to choosing between the different styles of Chinese and Japanese porcelain, particularly in the Chinese where the dynasties, the reign-marks and the French names all seem to add to the confusion. We can, however, get over this hurdle by simplifying. The Chinese decorated their porcelain in three main ways: blue and white, polychromes and monochromes, all sufficiently distinct to be easily identified. The Japanese copied the Chinese decorations to begin with, but later they developed a style of their own.

One of the aims of this book is to describe these different types of decoration and to aid the collector in choosing which he prefers. Though in the main we have confined its scope to the Ming and Ch'ing dynasties in China, as the wares of the earlier dynasties, with the exception of some modest examples, are now almost entirely museum pieces, and to the seventeenth, eighteenth and nineteenth centuries in Japan, we have occasionally looked back into earlier periods from which the later shapes and decorations have derived.

Once the collector is able to classify roughly Chinese and Japanese porcelain, he will find that he has an advantage over the collector of European porcelain, for the output of the Eastern industries was so much vaster than that of the West; from the seventeenth century onwards, fleets of ships of the different East India companies brought innumerable quantities of Chinese Export porcelain to Europe. To quote Addison once more: 'In her china-room were piles of plates and dishes and pyramids of cups and saucers, reaching from the floor to the ceiling.' This was the state of many rooms in country houses, even at Hampton Court, where Macaulay tells us: 'Mary (wife of William of Orange) acquired at the Hague a taste for Chinese porcelain and amused herself by forming a vast collection. . . .' From the quantity of Chinese Export available we could, almost, should we wish, do the same today.

Because it had to travel so far this Chinese Export porcelain was known as *Vases of the Sea*, for it included vases of all sizes among its cargo. Japanese porcelain arrived in Europe later in the seventeenth century than the Chinese, but there is a great quantity of it still to hand and it is usually more moderately priced. Chinese porcelain prices naturally vary, but reign-marks are unreliable, as the Chinese were in the habit of pre-dating these, sometimes by centuries, out of respect for former potters. We have, therefore, not included reign-marks in this book, preferring to leave the reader to consult the many authorities on the Far East who do so. We have, however, tried to interest collectors in Chinese symbols and the Chinese way of life through the objects described, so that their enjoyment in possession may be the greater. Such enjoyment was surely experienced by Dr Johnson and Horace Walpole. The Doctor, we are told, bought an oriental teapot of ample proportions, though it did not satisfy his unquenchable thirst, as he was in the habit of drinking no less than twenty cups at one sitting; whilst Horace Walpole, whose Chinese cups were of Lilliputian size, prized them so highly that he would allow no one to wash them up but himself, even though his hands were painful with gout. We can go one further and add to our porcelain (which fits as well as theirs in the eighteenth century, into our modern rooms of today) objects in bronze, jade, ivory and lacquer that will enable us to bring the Orient into our home.

The photographs of the objects are due to the courtesy of Mrs L. M. Chassaud, Miss Muriel Taylor and Mr George Horan, of *Oriental Antiques Ltd*, 28b St Christopher's Place, London W1. We also wish to express our heartfelt thanks to these collectors for their invaluable help, both during the writing and the revision of this book.

The Chinese Dynasties

Earlier Dynasties

SHANG-YIN	1766(?)–1122(?) B.C.	SUI	589–618
CHOU	1122(?)–221 B.C.	T'ANG	618–906
CH'IN	221–206 B.C.	THE FIVE DYNASTIES	907–960
HAN	206 B.C.–A.D. 220	SUNG	960–1279
THE SIX DYNASTIES	220–589	YUAN	1280–1368

Ming   1368–1644
Reigns

Hung Wu	1368–1398	Hung Chih	1488–1505
Chien Wen	1399–1402	Cheng Te	1506–1521
Yung Lo	1403–1424	Chia Ching	1522–1566
Hung Hsi	1425	Lung Ch'ing	1567–1572
Hsüan Te	1426–1435	Wan Li	1573–1619
Cheng T'ung	1436–1449	T'ai Ch'ang	1620
Ch'ing T'ai	1450–1457	T'ien Ch'i	1621–1627
T'ien Shun	1457–1464	Ch'ung Cheng	1628–1643
Ch'eng Hua	1465–1487		

Ch'ing   1644–1912
Reigns

Shun Chih	1644–1661	Tao Kuang	1821–1850
K'ang Hsi	1662–1722	Hsien Feng	1851–1861
Yung Cheng	1723–1735	T'ung Chih	1862–1873
Ch'ien Lung	1736–1795	Kuang Hsu	1874–1908
Chia-Ching	1796–1820	Hsüan Tung	1909–1912

Chinese Republic   1912

Introduction

Opening a door onto the East

What do we see if we hold a Chinese vase in our hands? Bright painted decoration in a whole range of enamel colours, standing out hard and clear on the milky-white translucent porcelain. But look a little bit closer. These overglaze enamels tell their stories of Chinese legends and beliefs; this hawthorn is a symbol of Spring; that old man with a beard is the god of Longevity; that dragon floating on a cloud brings rain when needed.

How exciting it must have been for Europeans at the beginning of the seventeenth century to learn what Chinamen looked like, how they dressed and in what setting they lived – to learn as much about Chinese customs, manners and philosophy from porcelain as they were able to do from books or pictures. The very substance itself was a delight. Nothing like it had ever been seen in Europe before. This magical-looking substance was in reality a mixture of two rock-like elements, china-clay and china-stone, fired together at a very high temperature, so that it became clear, white and translucent, a perfect background for the brilliance of coloured enamel decorations. Naturally the European potters were full of admiration and longed to produce this substance for themselves.

How did this china come to be known as porcelain? When first introduced into Europe at the end of the sixteenth century it was compared to the polished surface of the cowrie shell or 'porcellana', because its curved upper surface was supposed to resemble the rounded back of a 'porcella' or little hog. The Scottish, indeed, spoke of it occasionally as 'pigs'. But although porcelain was in the air from 1711 onwards, with factories opening all over Europe, these factories never approached Chinese production. This is not surprising, for the Chinese porcelain industry had been supplying the Arab world from as early as the fourteenth century and had grown to employ, so it is said, as many as a million workers in the Chinese city of Ching-tê-chên by the reign of that famous patron of the arts, the Emperor K'ang Hsi (1622–1722).

A vivid picture of the city at this period is drawn for us by Père D'Entrecolles, the Jesuit priest who was such an authority on Chinese porcelain, in a letter dated September 1712, to a friend in Paris:

King-tê-Tching is estimated to contain 18000 households, the population is said to number over a million souls. When passing along you seem to be in the midst of a Fair. Even the blind and maimed can make a living by grinding colours. Approaching at night-fall, the scene reminds one of a burning city in flames or of a huge furnace with many vent-holes.

Longfellow corroborates this impression in his *Keramos*:

> And bird-like poised on balanced wing,
> Above the town of King-tê-Tching,
> A burning town or seeming so,
> Three thousand furnaces that glow
> Incessantly, and fill the air
> With smoke uprising gyre on gyre
> And painted by the lurid glare
> Of jets and flashes of red fire.

It is hardly astonishing with this enormous output that Eastern porcelain, including the Japanese, is still to be found in surprisingly large quantities today. You could, for instance, put together, by buying the individual pieces separately, a whole dinner-service of Chinese export ware of the late eighteenth century, for less than it would cost you to buy a dinner-service in say, nineteenth century English bone china.

Miniature replica in pink coral of Chinese Commemorative columns, such as can be s
outside Chinese Temples or Palaces. Engraved with dragons and clouds, with mythical ani
crouching on top. Height: 13¼ ins. Circa eighteenth cent

China and Japan . . . How far away they sound! But once you have one or two pieces of Eastern Export porcelain in your own home, your delight in them will probably lead you to want to know more about them. Confucius tells us that to appreciate it is necessary, first, to understand. Follow his advice and soon your treasures will become for you, as they are for the Chinese, 'a solace for the eyes' in moments of leisure.

It is hard for us westerners to understand the importance of porcelain to the Chinese. There is a legend that on one occasion the Chinese Emperor sent models from Peking to be copied at Ching-tê-chên, but skilled as the workmen were, the reproductions remained unsatisfactory. The Emperor promised rewards and threatened punishments to no avail. Finally one of the workmen, in desperation, threw himself into the furnace and perished, but the ware that was being baked came out so perfect that the Emperor was satisfied and the unlucky workman became the 'God of the Furnaces'. Such devotion to porcelain-making may be taken as symbolic of the feelings of the whole nation. Even about the Government we read: 'Our successors, looking back to the present time, may know from the porcelain produced the kind of Government which we had.' It was said by T'ang, the successor of the famous director Ts'ang, under K'ang Hsi, whose able management resulted in one of the most brilliant periods of Chinese ceramics in the seventy years between 1680 and 1750, that 'when Ts'ang was in charge of the factory the god laid his finger on the designs and protected the porcelain in the kilns, so that it naturally came out perfect.'

In his *T'ao Shuo*, Chu Yen, the poet who was stationed at Ching-tê-chên from 1767 to 1774, writes about his book on porcelain and pottery: 'This book should be widely distributed throughout the Empire and many will be delighted with the perusal of its contents.' No doubt many Chinese readers were so delighted, and reading some of his poetic descriptions it is easy to share in their pleasure, for no image, however grandiose, could exaggerate the strength of their feelings for these exquisite objects:

The thousand peaks have been despoiled of their bright colours for the decoration of the bowls. Therefore let us take them out at midnight and collect the falling dew.

Or take this verse sent with the presentation of teacups to the Emperor Ch'ien Lung (1736–95):

Like bright moons cunningly carved and dyed with Spring,
Like curling disks of thinnest ice filled with green clouds,
Like ancient moss-eaten bronze mirrors lying upon the mat,
Like tender lotus-leaves full of dew-drops floating on the river-side. . . .

He tells us that the green glaze was called the 'colour of the distant hills' and that Ch'ing green was a favourite for harmonizing with the different kinds of tea and wine, while for the banqueting table white painted porcelain was the best. Could there be any better illustration of porcelain being part of the very life of the Chinese? And how about this for a description of colour: 'The reds were so spectacular that some people thought that rubies had been crushed in with the glaze'?

No beautiful sight or sound eluded the poet when describing porcelain:

Blue as the sky, brilliant as a mirror,
Thin as paper, resonant as a musical stone.

Even the rank-and-file of the Chinese would often use pictorial language to describe the colours in which they painted their porcelain. Who but they would describe bright-speckled blue as the 'colour of a robin's egg', or compare yellow to a sunflower, or red vases with a happy fault in pigment to 'peaches' bloom' or dark red to 'ox blood'? Materials also came in for graphic descriptions, such as shagreen, which is described as 'chicken's skin'.

The greatest masterpieces in porcelain were reserved for the Emperor and the Mandarins, but even the humblest scribe was given exquisite small objects to put his writing materials into, that their beauty might persuade him to persevere with his craft. Not so kind was the idea of presenting a porcelain pillow to the scholar, so that he wouldn't over-sleep and neglect his studies.

Chinese art is closely bound up with religion. In the state religion there was no priesthood. The Emperor was the 'Son of Heaven' and as he worshipped heaven so the people worshipped him. When worshipping heaven the Emperor wore azure robes like the sky, when the earth, yellow robes, when the sun, red, and when the moon, white. No wonder that the colours on Chinese porcelain are so exquisite! But if the colours are outstanding, man himself is less so, anyhow after the end of the sixteenth century. The Chinese had too much humility to believe that God created man in His own image. Nature was their great hero. In Nature they might contemplate the grandeur of all things created, and Nature itself could assume semi-divine forms. In the designs, therefore, man is often less important than the landscape which is his setting. Heroes are depicted, but more popular is the heroism of a faithful wife, father or son who accepts adversity with resignation. The authority of the head of the family is, however, apparently unquestioned, even after death, for the Chinese have a great belief in ancestor worship. It was an ancient custom to put objects into the tombs of the dead, which they thought might be useful to them beyond the grave. Ceramic replicas of musicians, dancers, dogs, oxen, horses, pigs, hens and ducks, all found their way into these tombs. The famous T'ang horses are an example of these 'mortuary' figures, as they were called, but it was not until the early twentieth century that this strange world under the earth was revealed by excavation.

Many of the designs on Chinese porcelain are symbolic and have a tremendous significance for the people. Dragons are frequently to be met with, and there is a belief that should the dragon on a bowl have five claws, the bowl would have been commissioned by the Imperial Court or household, if not by the Emperor, himself.

The Chinese Repository, *Notices of Natural History*, tells us:

There are three chief species of dragon. The 'lung', which is the most powerful and inhabits the sky; the 'li', which is harmless and lives in the ocean, and the 'chiao', which is scaly and resides in marshes and dens in the mountains.

The lung, 'Lord of the Skies', as he was named in Chinese mythology, must have been a fearsome-looking beast, judging by one description of him: 'Head of a camel, the horns of a deer, eyes of a rabbit, ears of a cow, neck of a snake, belly of a frog, scales of a carp, claws of a hawk and palm of a tiger.' This almost sounds as if he had been brewed in the witches' cauldron in *Macbeth*. The description continues: 'On each side of its mouth are whiskers and a beard hangs under its chin, where also is placed a bright pearl. Its breath proceeds from the mouth like a cloud; being sometimes changed into water, at other times into fire; its voice is like the jingling of copper pans.' This rather terrifying description seems to be modified in Japan, where the dragon was supposed, according to Okakura, the author of *The Awakening of Japan*, to be the genius of strength and goodness, 'the spirit of change, therefore of life itself'.

In his *Chinese Porcelain*, W. G. Gulland observes that very often dragons appear to be emitting a pearl (chiu) from their mouths. The pearl has been prized from time immemorial by the Chinese, who named it the 'concrete essence of the moon' and 'the night-shining pearl'. A serpent must possess a pearl before it can become a dragon, for the pearl is a charm to avert tempests, floods and fire. Even the Buddhist lion condescends to play with a ball (chu). If he loses the 'chu' he is said to lose his life.

Dragons are more frequently to be met with on porcelain than the three other important creatures, the unicorn (or Ch'i-lin), the phoenix and the tortoise – all supreme emblems of benevolence and good. The unicorn is held in the highest affection of all four, being, we are told by Mayers in *The Chinese Reader's Manual*, 'the noblest form of animal creation, the emblem of perfect good'. It is sometimes called the 'dragon horse' or 'Kylin' (Ch'i-lin) and is not unlike a large stag. The male has one main horn proceeding out of its forehead, the tip of which is fleshy so it is stamped as an animal unfit for war. It never shows itself these days, because mankind has become too degenerate.

The phoenix, resembling a pheasant, and adorned with everything that is beautiful amongst birds, is the symbol of the Empress. It is supposed to appear only in times of peace and prosperity.

The tortoise, the only down to earth character in this galaxy of fantasy, nevertheless holds its own because it symbolizes the universe. In *Lamaism*, Waddell tells us that 'its dome-shaped back represents the vault of the sky; its belly the earth . . . and its fabulous longevity leads to its being considered imperishable'.

The animals, fabulous and otherwise, appearing on porcelain, are too numerous to mention. Among those to be seen most frequently are the tiger, respected by the Chinese as the God of Gambling, the hare, sacred to the moon, the horse, emblem of wisdom, the cat, a symbol of poverty, because it catches the rats and mice who appear when a house is in a state of decay, the ass, symbolical, as in the West, of stupidity, the stork, emblem of longevity, and the crane, the most celebrated bird in Chinese legend. The parrot, also, has a curious legend attached to it. W. G. Gulland tells us that in the province of Kiangsi, where stood the city of Ching-tê-chên, a speaking parrot warned a pearl merchant that his wife's intrigues were on the point of ruining him. In this province, therefore, this bird was looked upon as a warning to women to be faithful to their husbands. Of the fish, which are supposed to keep away demons and evil spirits, carp and perch are the two species most frequently to be met with on porcelain.

Among the insects the butterfly is supposed to be a sign of conjugal felicity – W. G. Gulland compares him to 'a kind of Chinese cupid'. The story goes that a young student, running after a butterfly, strayed into a garden where he saw the magistrate's daughter. He was so charmed by her beauty that, though she was far above him in station, he succeeded, by working hard, in winning her for his wife.

As well as creatures from the animal kingdom, plants also play an important part in Chinese symbolism. There is a Chinese saying that the pine, bamboo and plum trees are like three friends, because they keep green in cold weather. The pine and bamboo trees are emblems of longevity, as is the peach, which is also an emblem of marriage. A figure sitting under a palm tree is a symbol of retired life, free from the turmoils of the world, just as a man with faggots represents a secluded life in the country, and a man with a net, the same by the sea.

Of the fruits and flowers, the orange is a symbol of good fortune and the gourd is said to ward off evil influence. The peach-blossom, also, was a flower placed at doorways to prevent evil from entering. The prunus, peony, lotus and chrysanthemum symbolize the four seasons, but the drawing of flowers on porcelain can be misleading, for Nature is not always strictly copied.

Apart from animal and vegetable symbolism there were numerous emblems and charms used by the gods and goddesses, such as the bell, to awaken the attention of the gods to their worshippers, and the fan, which has a curious story attached to it, told us by Sir John Davis.

One day the philosopher Chung-li met a woman fanning her husband's grave. She explained to him that her husband had forbidden her to marry till the earth of his grave was dry, whereupon the philosopher helped her to fan it and was well scolded by his own wife, who protested that the woman must be a 'monster of insensitivity'. To test his wife's loyalty, the philosopher pretended to be dead, but when she decided to marry again as quickly as she could, he came rapidly to life.

The gods and goddesses themselves are very often represented, especially the God of Longevity and the Eight Immortals. These Eight Immortals are legendary beings of the Taoist Sect and are often depicted on porcelain, as well as being made in figures, either standing or seated. The chief of them is Chung-li Ch'uan, said to have lived under the Chou dynasty (1122–249 B.C.) and to have obtained the secret of the elixir of life. His emblem is a fan with which he is said to revive the souls of the dead, and he is supposed to be the very philosopher in the story of the fan, told above. Four of the Immortals are patron saints, living around A.D. 800. Lu-Tung-Pin, who holds the Taoist fly-brush in his right hand, is the patron saint of barbers; Ts'ao Kuo-chin, whose emblem is a pair of castanets, of the theatrical profession; Han Hsiang-Tsu (emblem the flute) of the musicians, and Lan Ts'ai-ho (emblem a flower-basket) of the florists.

Of the other three, Chang Kuo-lao is a wanderer, the ancestor of the happy vagabond, with a kind of musical instrument in the shape of a bamboo tube or drum with two rods to beat it, and Ho-Hsien-ku, whose emblem is the lotus, assists in house management. The most curious legend of all is told about Li-T'ieh kuai, represented as a beggar leaning on an iron staff. Having magical powers he was often summoned to Celestial Regions, but once, when his spirit was away on one of these journeys his disciple, thinking he was dead, burned his body, and when he returned the only body he could find to inhabit was that of a beggar. His emblem, a pilgrim's gourd, sometimes shown with a scroll escaping, shows his power to set the spirit free from his body.

Apart from the God of Longevity the gods and goddesses include the Goddess of Mercy, the God of Wealth and the God of Literature. Of these, Kuanyin, the Goddess of Mercy, is often represented in figures of *blanc de chine*, sometimes with a child in her arms, and has been compared to the Virgin Mary. There was no god in China more universally worshipped than the god of wealth, usually accompanied by two attendants, and particularly adored by poor people and gamblers. The God of Literature has two human forms, Wen Ch'ang and K'uei. As Wen Ch'ang, he is a handsome man, usually in a sitting posture; as K'uei, he is very ugly, almost a demon, with a head having horned projections. He is usually depicted holding a pen and a book on which are written four Chinese characters, 'Heaven decides literary success'.

What of the painters whose business it was to reproduce all this complicated symbolism? In China there was a great affinity between poetry and painting even as early as the Sung dynasty, around 1127–1279. Painting was indeed sometimes called 'a voiceless poem', and Mario Prodan, in *An Introduction to Chinese Art*, tells the story of the Emperor who asked his painters to illustrate the verse:

> I return from trampling upon flowers
> And the hooves of my horse smell sweet.

He awarded the prize to the painter showing two butterflies hovering around a horse's hooves. As in the poem, the painting shows a subtle sense of the exquisite.

In spite of this, painting on porcelain was never esteemed as highly as poetry, because it was largely considered a mechanical occupation, intended for copying designs which had been in use for a thousand years. Perhaps, because of this, the most successful decorations on Chinese porcelain, such as insects, birds, fruit, flowers and ornamental patterns, are those where perspective and shading are not important. Originally the Chinese almost had a fear of perspective, and when it was once used by a Jesuit, were convinced that he had summoned some magic art to produce the effect. His picture was immediately condemned. Davis tells us that the Chinese mandarins considered the shadow of the nose as a great imperfection in the face and supposed it to have been placed there by accident. But later, in the early part of the eighteenth century, the Chinese did consent to accept instruction in perspective from two Jesuit priests.

Painting may have been considered inferior to poetry, but we find Père D'Entrecolles, the best informed of the Jesuits, laying down a high standard for painting on porcelain: 'For painting flowers, birds, fishes or water-plants and living objects, generally the study of nature is the first requisite. . . . In the decoration of porcelain the correct canons of art should be followed. The design should be taken from the patterns of old brocades and embroidery, the colours from a garden as seen in springtime from a parlour.' Nevertheless, painting in the Ming dynasty, preceding the Ch'ing (the dynasty to which Père D'Entrecolles is referring), was much more spontaneous and vigorous, because the Ming industry was on a smaller scale and there was less division of labour. Speaking about the factory of Ching-tê-chên, Père D'Entrecolles tells us that one man painted outlines only, another flowers only, another animals and another humans, while a different set of workmen filled in the designs with washes: 'One workman has the sole office of forming the first coloured rim which we see round the edge of porcelain. Another traces the flowers which a third colours, this artist paints the water and the mountains and the birds and other animals. . . . I am told that a piece of porcelain has passed through the hands of seventy workmen. . . .'

Tastes differ. Both the Ming and the Ch'ing porcelain have their devotees, today as they had in the past. People, at all times and in all places have dreamed of creating a Utopia. Distance lends charm and China, in the seventeenth and eighteenth centuries, perhaps because it was still largely unexplored territory, fired the Western imagination. In this faraway land it seemed that the sun was always shining, that folk sat under trees drinking wine and philosophizing in a state of untroubled calm. Coleridge's dream of Kubla Khan, who reigned during the dynasty of Yuan (1280–1368) at the time when Marco Polo visited China, also catches something of this atmosphere:

> And there were gardens bright with sinuous rills
> Where blossomed many an incense-bearing tree. . . .

Surely a reflection of this dream can be ours today, as we handle these exquisite pieces of the Far East, for as Chu Yen tells us: 'A minute's handling is better than a page of description.'

CHINA

Chinese export Porcelain

Please do not send any more dragons

Père D'Entrecolles, that great French Jesuit authority on Chinese porcelain, writes: 'Those of the Mandarins who understand the Western genius have tried to reproduce it, and they have asked me to get new and interesting designs from Europe, so that they will have something bizarre to offer to the Emperor.' But the Emperor also had his own ideas. He wished to have 'something bizarre' to offer to Europe. Thus from the seventeenth century onwards the Chinese began to aim at producing special objects which they hoped would please their European customers. This was known as *Chinese Export Porcelain*, for the best Imperial porcelain was never allowed out of China unless the Emperor or the mandarins made a personal gift, such as that which K'ang Hsi sent to Louis XIV of France as a gesture of friendship.

Though a quantity of Ming porcelain had already found its way to Europe in the first half of the seventeenth century, the greatest flow of export porcelain belongs to the Ch'ing dynasty from 1644 to 1912. When we read how this precious porcelain was handled, it seems almost a miracle that there is so much of it available in junk shops and street markets today. For example, William Hickey, travelling in the East between 1749 and 1775, wrote, after a visit to the English Hong (depots of East India Companies) in Canton: 'I was aggrieved at my friend McClintock taking too long to finish his meal. He just pushed the table over, and when I expressed my displeasure at his action, the young pickle exclaimed: "I never suffer the servants to have the trouble of removing the equipage. I throw the whole (crockery) out of the window or downstairs. They can easily produce another batch from the steward's warehouse."'

Careless as this attitude may appear it was nothing out of the ordinary, for before this date the porcelain had been used as ballast to make flooring in the holds of ships, spice, silk and tea being considered the important merchandise. Indeed from the very start of its journey, the life of this precious porcelain seems to have been precarious. From the Chinese factories the wares were shipped to Canton, where we learn that: 'The bed of the stream appeared to be paved with countless fragments of porcelain, mute glittering records of many generations of potters.'

However, against this carefree attitude to the wares, we have the testimony of the Emperor's chief overseer at Ching-tê-chên. Completely overwhelmed by the flow of export porcelain, he writes: 'Though a broken-down horse, I put forth all my strength. . . .' He certainly seems to have done so, judging by the pieces which have survived. The first pieces to be exported were the blue and white. These were followed by the polychromes – i.e., painting over the glaze in enamel colours amongst which were the *famille verte* and *famille rose*. This 'pink family' easily surpassed its rival, the 'green family' in popularity, and the demand for it was so great that the collector's search today is still very rewarding.

As these coloured wares were so popular, the beginning of the nineteenth century saw a new line in export. The accommodating Chinese, thinking that the European craze for blue and white might be on the wane, painted over the already existing blue and white in bright enamel colours. The mongrel of Chinese decoration which resulted is known as 'clobbering', and its quaintness still has a certain appeal. The Chinese desire to please even led them to tackle the intricacies of the arms of noble European families in the seventeenth and eighteenth centuries. This particular line of export was known as 'Armorial Porcelain'.

All these wares, after being sent down the river to the Port of Canton, were trans-shipped to the various European countries. A writer of the time gives a colourful picture of what this river looked like:

Junks from the East Indies, Philippine cargo-boats, ferries, barbers' boats, fortune-tellers' vessels, boats loaded with theatrical performers. Imagine a city afloat, and that would convey a very correct idea of the incessant movement, the subdued noises, the life, the gaiety of the river.

For the Europeans, trade was by no means all gaiety. The Chinese customs officers expected to receive clocks and mechanical gadgets as presents. The 'Hong' merchants, specially appointed to deal with foreigners, claimed a rake-off from the eunuchs acting for the Emperor, as well as from the European merchants. As one merchant wrote to his colleague: 'S— is like all other Chinese you deal with, except in one particular, he is an *honourable* scoundrel.'

Bearing in mind the dissimilarity between the Chinese and European civilizations, it is indeed remarkable that the Chinese were able to reproduce European subjects to please their customers. Some of their porcelain workers were Christian converts – there was a Jesuit Mission at Ching-tê-chên and also at Canton. This 'Jesuit China' depicted scenes from the Old and New Testaments, though sometimes the Chinese made full use of their poetic licence, as when, to gratify the Dutch, they painted in Dutch sailors witnessing the Crucifixion and the Resurrection.

Having so many gods and goddesses of their own it was easy for the Chinese to enter into the spirit of Greek mythology. The Toilet of Venus, Venus amongst the clouds, Adonis, Psyche and Cupid, Hercules, and Europa and the Bull were all reproduced, though swathings of pink and orange cloth were cast about them, and even Cupid was decently clad.

Masonic decoration was also attempted, with the sun in splendour, the planets and the moon; and columns and archways on bowls whose borders were usually blue with gold stars.

Sometimes the European picture galleries provided designs. English,

Fine Plate made for East India Company, with
European decoration. Ch'ien Lung Period.

French and Italian eighteenth century paintings were copied, among them Lancret's *Cherry Pickers* and Watteau's *Carnival in Venice*; as well as rustic patterns from copper-plate engravings, for instance, European amateur musicians in a Chinese landscape.

With so many ships calling at Canton it was only natural that their officers would order designs of vessels to appear on punch bowls, mugs and flagons. The Chinese had plenty of opportunity to execute these as ships had sometimes to wait for months at Canton. Du Halde, an eighteenth century writer, tell us: 'The River seems like a large wood, by the multitude of vessels which are there.' Shipping scenes on the Chinese coast, with European figures in eighteenth century costume, were popular, and also Dutch harbour scenes.

In sport, the hunting-scene designs show how strange this was to the Chinese mind. For example, a foxhound can be represented by almost any kind of dog. As well as these European scenes, there were also many Chinese ones and old favourites, such as the dragon, were well represented. We learn, also, that even the overwhelming desire to please of the Chinese was not able to satisfy all customers. Thus we get one 'foreign devil', as the Chinese nicknamed Europeans, writing: 'Please do not send any more dragons. Let us have some flowers instead.'

Towards the end of the eighteenth century the Chinese had acquired new and important customers, namely the 'flowery flag devils', as they called the Americans. Within a few years of the War of American Independence, the American ship trade with China had exceeded that of the English with the East India Company. This American enterprise called forth the admiration of the English statesman, Edmund Burke: 'Neither the perseverance of Holland, nor the activity of France, nor the sagacity of England ever carried this most perilous mode of hardy industry to the extent to which it has been pushed by this most recent people.'

The Chinese were just as obliging to their American customers as they were to the Europeans. The American eagle was copied, sometimes with

35

an olive branch and sometimes with a scroll, 'In God We Trust', in its
beak. They made designs for Martha Washington's Patriotic Service,
with a wreath of leaves and 'M.W.' in the centre. They also decorated
flagons with Washington's portrait, and commemorated his memorial
service with an American eagle, together with a weeping willow.

The European craze for porcelain collecting finds its counterpart in
an American nineteenth century writer, Alice Morse Earle, who tells
us how she scoured the American countryside, knocking on farm-house
doors in the hope of unearthing ceramics. This enterprising lady also
speaks of the unusual methods employed by some Americans when buying porcelain:

Many a pretty blue Canton teapot and cup and saucer, or a great ringing
punch bowl came home from China in return for the hoarded egg-money, the
inherited Spanish dollars or the proceeds of the Year's spinning and weaving.
The venture was a hundred years ago a gentle commercial speculation in which
all Puritan womanhood longed to join. Friends and neighbours were socially
allowed to join with the shipmaster in his risks and profits. These ventures
brought in good profits and still allowed the shipmasters to be rich. Women
became assailed by a gambling obsession, sold their gold beads, their spring
lambs, and got in return tea, spices and china. Some fair maids bought, through
a venture, their bridal finery.

Frequently the china was sold direct from the vessel on a wharf alongside.
How truly Oriental the old china-ware must have seemed to the Boston and
Salem dames when they tiptoed down on the old wharf in wooden clogs! Truly
we of today have lost the romance of colonial shipping, when we know not the
ship nor scarcely the country from whence cometh our stores. Tall coffee pots
with straight spouts looking like light-houses with bow sprits, short clumsy
teapots with twisted handles. In past years, when roast pig and giant turkeys
were served, these great platters held their steaming trophies of turkeys. . . .

Was it the 'foreign devil' or the 'flowery flag devil' who came off best
in the race for *Chinese Export Porcelain*? Probably they both broke about
even, but it would take too long to count which of them has the most
dragons.

Blue and White

There's a joy without canker or cark,
There's a pleasure eternally new,
'Tis to gloat on the glaze and the mark
Of china that's ancient and blue.

ANDREW LANG

In *Punch* magazine, dated 1874, we find a cartoon by Du Maurier, making fun of the craze for blue and white Chinese porcelain. A wife is nursing a Chinese blue and white teapot. Her husband says: 'I think you might let me nurse that pot a little now.' Whereupon the wife replies: 'But you had it to yourself all the morning!'

More than three centuries lie between this cartoon and the first bowls of blue and white given to Sir Thomas Trenchard in 1506 by Philip of Austria, but this was a unique treasure, for it was not until the middle of the sixteenth century that this precious porcelain began to trickle into Europe. From then onwards large quantities, first of Ming and then of Ch'ing porcelain, almost entirely blue and white, flowed steadily towards the West, gradually attaining the popularity caricatured in the cartoon.

The term *blue and white* is applied to the unbaked paste which is glazed and fired, once only, at a high temperature and painted under the glaze. The Chinese had already begun to make this type of porcelain as early as the fourteenth century for home consumption and for export to the Arab countries. This was during the Ming dynasty, which began in 1368

37

and lasted till 1644. Ming *blue and white* is often of a greenish or bluish shade, instead of pure white.

By the fifteenth century *blue and white* had already come into its own in China. A new style of decoration had also arisen. The method of painting in bold splashes of colour had been replaced by one in which the outlines were carefully drawn and the spaces filled in with a uniform wash. There were large dishes with unglazed bases, decorated with lotus flowers and leaves, tied with ribbon or with ribbons streaming in the wind. There were also massive jars used as food containers. The early sixteenth century saw many smaller articles, such as those for writing-tables, ink-slabs and boxes with covers. The *blue and white* of this period has always been prized for the brilliance of its blue decoration. Apart from this, the potters also produced a brilliant dark-purplish blue which is typical of the period. But in Wan-Li's reign (1573–1617) this blue was already beginning to deteriorate and only occasionally attained its former brilliance. The importance of Wan-Li's reign for *blue and white*, however, cannot be too much stressed, because a great part of the pieces known today belong to this era, although collectors may have to search far and wide to find them.

During this period, a new and lighter style of decoration in a silvery blue was developed. This seems to foreshadow the lighter styles of decoration of the Ch'ing period. By this time the supply of export pieces to Europe was immense, judging by the large number that have survived. Some of these pieces are skilfully and vigorously decorated with motifs such as ducks and water-weeds, spotted deer and landscapes and sometimes human figures. Often a branch, intended to represent longevity, encloses these. Wan-Li was the last great Emperor of the Ming dynasty. This period will always be remembered for the vigour of its decoration and its firm sketching, but though its beauty grew to full maturity it lacked sophistication, although it made up for this in fantasy. Examples are the flower-jars with dragons sporting amongst clouds or in the waves of a rising tide, or dragons playing with lotus

38

Blue and white K'ang Hsi Beaker. Height: 10

flowers. The blue painting of the Ming is not graduated or shaded and has a powerful decorative effect in large objects, such as jars and vases in which the period excelled. Among the flowers, lilies and poppies are often to be found.

After Wan-Li's death in 1617 the Ming Empire began to disintegrate, the strict Imperial control of ceramics became much looser, and without this supervision the independent potters were freer to indulge in their own designs. These less restricted designs belong to what is known as the *Transition Period*. In this period, which lasted roughly from 1620–62, the blue has a slightly purplish tint which has been described as 'violets in milk'. The painters show a keener sense of natural beauty, landscape begins to dominate and is no longer a background to human figures. As the painters were given full rein for their fantasy. This was also the period of the development of stories in pictures which was to reach the height of its popularity under the reign of K'ang Hsi. There were illustrations of fairy tales, also stories of popular heroes and beautiful maidens. The device of representing a dream by a separate enclosed picture, Walter Mitty style, is also used. For example, a civil servant, having dined too well, has fallen asleep and on the other side of the vase, his dream, in which he bursts into the garden of his lady-love, is depicted.

After the short prelude of the reign of Shun Chih (1644–61) the Ch'ing dynasty burst into its full glory under the long reign of K'ang Hsi (1662–1722). The blue here was of a purity, depth and brilliance in its sapphire colouring that raises it to the summit of *blue and white* porcelain. Though it has lost the spontaneous vigour and freedom of the Ming, it has gained symmetry and balance in decorative effects. The glaze is faultless, the paste of the highest quality and the pieces are of a luminous azure blue that would be hard to equal. Père D'Entrecolles describes this development very vividly:

A beautiful blue colour appears on porcelain, after having been lost for some time. When the colour is first painted on it is pale black; when it is dry and the glaze has been put on it, it disappears entirely and the porcelain seems quite white, the colour being buried under the glaze. But the fire makes it appear in all its beauty, almost in the same way as the natural heat of the sun makes the most beautiful butterflies with all their tints, come out of their eggs.

In *blue and white* the styles of decoration are immensely varied. Here we find deities and emperors in suitably grand surroundings, down to a simple twig of prunus or other symbolic plant, such as the sweet-flag, which is said to ward off evil spirits. The decoration includes the phoenix, chrysanthemums, peonies, lotus-blossom, dragons, slender ladies, children parodying the staid occupations of their elders and the famous hawthorn pattern. This flower is not really a hawthorn but the blossom of the plum (or prunus) which, perhaps because it produced its blossom before its leaves, symbolizes spring. A favourite motif often to be seen on jars is the falling blossom of the plum against a background of cracked ice, signifying the death of winter and the coming of spring. These jars with the prunus motif were often given as Chinese New Year gifts. There were also vases decorated with landscapes of pine-trees, storks and deer, which are the usual emblems of immortality, and ginger-jars, one of the most popular forms of *blue and white* – a form which has been copied up to the present day. These ginger-jars, which were more often used for storing tea, were also part of the New Year ceremony. One friend would buy the very best jar that he could find, fill it with tea and present it to another friend. This friend, in his turn, would present a similar highly-prized jar to him. They would then drink tea together. When the tea was finished, they would solemnly exchange jars, so that each one would get back the jar of his own choice.

In his *Outlines of Chinese Symbolism and Art Motives*, C. A. S. Williams tells us that 'gazing on plums to quench thirst is the Chinese equivalent to 'sour grapes', because the soldiers of the resourceful General Ts'ao Ts'ao (A.D. 155–220) when thirsty, were told to look at a distant grove of plum-trees, which made their mouths water.' Luckily our mouths need not water as we gaze at these inviting Ch'ing vases, for some Ch'ing *blue and white* is well within our reach today.

Large blue and white vase.
K'ang Hsi Period.

One delightful example of nineteenth century Ch'ing, which we found was a large vase decorated with dragons, underneath which were some little carp. The carp were looking up at the dragon far above them, as if they wished to come higher up on the vase. This is surely the Eastern equivalent of our proverb: 'Try, try, try again!'

As, during the reign of K'ang Hsi the nuances of blue colour were endless, it is quite a good plan to take in your pocket a small piece of genuine *blue and white* when you visit the auction room or the shop, to help you to keep your eye in.

After K'ang Hsi's reign large quantities of *blue and white* still continued to be made for export, but were on the whole inferior to K'ang Hsi pieces.

42

Ginger Jar, blue and white, with pheasants perched on flowering branches. Diameter: 34 ins. Height: 15 ins. Late nineteenth century.

The Chinese made many objects purely to please their Western customers, for which they had no use themselves, such as cups with handles, sauce-boats and punch-bowls. Anyone who has eaten in a Chinese restaurant knows that the cups are usually without handles and that sauces are not served separately.

When you are in a picture gallery you will often notice pieces of *blue and white* that the artists of the seventeenth and eighteenth centuries have painted into their pictures. This proves how Chinese porcelain had found a niche for itself in European decoration. In the nineteenth century Whistler, although he did not actually put *blue and white* into his pictures, as his subjects were unsuitable for it, was so keen on this china that, during the Boxer Rising, his only concern was that the *blue and white* porcelain should be spared. Rather sadistically, whilst everyone was worrying about the fate of the British in China, he exclaimed: 'All the Englishmen in the world are not worth one *blue and white* Chinese vase!'

Rossetti, his contemporary, was also enough of a *blue and white* fanatic to attract the attention of Du Maurier. In *Punch*, 1864, the cartoonist caricatures Rossetti deserting his guests at a dinner-party and rushing off to buy a piece of *blue and white*, for fear that it should be sold before he could get there. Rossetti is also honoured by Du Maurier in 1878, where he is drawn having supper at Scott's and tipping the contents of his food out of his *blue and white* plate in order to examine the mark underneath. On the other hand, Oscar Wilde, in his characteristic way, regretted that he 'could not live up to such china'.

We may not be as witty as Wilde, but with such a lot of this precious stuff around, it is not difficult to become, with a little 'Patience', to quote Gilbert:

> Such a judge of blue and white
> And other kinds of pottery
> From early Oriental
> Down to modern terra-cot-tery.

Ming Polychromes

An introduction to Ch'ing polychromes

The Ming dynasty saw the rise not only of *blue and white*, but also of the painting in enamel colours known as *polychromes*.

The three-coloured palette, the 'San ts'ai', began by being green, yellow and aubergine (a purplish brown). The ground decoration is often covered with a yellow glaze on which the green and aubergine are painted in various designs. Sometimes black is used with the other colours, or the design is sketched in black, which shows through the coloured enamel. The three-coloured palette of the Ming evolved in the Ch'ing dynasty, when it was painted onto unglazed porcelain, a process known as 'painting on the biscuit' – i.e., the paste after it had been baked but not glazed.

At Polesden Lacey in Surrey the stands of a pair of Buddhist lions are painted in this way, on the biscuit. The Buddhist lion is sometimes called the 'Dog of Fo', because it is found in stone mounting guard at the threshold of Buddhist temples, and as such is, according to Anderson in his *Catalogue of Japanese and Chinese Paintings in the British Museum*, 'by no means a formidable beast, despite its eyes and fierce countenance'. The lions in Polesden Lacey were exported to Europe at the end of the seventeenth century. They are in white and green enamel; one is playing with a cub, and the other with a brocade ball. As they were made chiefly for export, they have not only wide, smiling mouths but also eyes which when moved, actually shoot out of the head and back again.

The so-called five-coloured palette, the 'Wu ts'ai', or early *famille verte*, appeared in the reign of Chia-Ching (1522–66). It usually consisted

45

of red, green, yellow and blue, often to be found with a little added white. The Ming blue was under the glaze, unless used as a glaze itself, and it was not until the next dynasty, in the reign of K'ang Hsi, that the pleasant blue enamel over the glaze was added and the five-colour palette became the famous *famille verte*.

Famille Verte

'This porcelain is loaded with colours, and all this gay colouring of the enamels commends this porcelain to our rooms.' Thus Père D'Entrecolles describes the so-called five-coloured palette, on which green plays a leading part, known as the *famille verte*. Albert Jacquemart, the well-known nineteenth century French collector, claimed to have given the porcelain this name, for Chinese porcelain was first seriously studied in Europe by the French.

The *famille verte* derives from a late Ming style, taken up and developed by the potters in the reign of K'ang Hsi (1662–1722). The chief differences between the Ming five-coloured palette and *famille verte* are due to the disappearance of the turquoise and the substitution of the underglaze blue by a beautiful enamel which had scarcely been seen before. The green in *famille verte* varies from the heavy to the most delicate touches. It may practically cover the whole of a vase or bowl, or it may be used only as a slight spray of leaves amongst the other colours. Its shades are all important, for there are so many variations of green, as everyone knows who has dabbled in painting. The greens at which the K'ang Hsi potters aimed were all brilliant and clear; they had no use for clouded or dirty shades.

The background of the *famille verte* is of white glaze, against which the colours of the five palette show up very vividly. There are usually, apart from the green, a vivid red, often known as iron-red, over-glaze blue, yellow and aubergine, but other colours do sometimes intrude.

The early Ch'ing *famille verte* of K'ang Hsi has masses of dark green, described by Monkhouse as 'a leafy hue', and not much blue. As decoration, we find, amongst other designs, flowering-plants, phoenixes, graceful ladies and landscapes. The green of the *famille verte* lends itself, naturally, to the designing of trees. The graceful willow is the feminine tree. Slender Chinese ladies were said to have willow waists, and Chinese female dancers tried to imitate the movement of willow trees. The pine tree, because it is evergreen, was regarded as the symbols of longevity and the friend who remains constant in adversity. Very often a figure sitting under a palm tree, often to be found on *famille verte*, is a symbol of retired life, free from the turmoils of the world.

> Where my pathway came to an end
> By the rising waters covered,
> I sat me down to watch the shapes
> In the mist that over it hovered.

The poem illustrates the thinker and the philosopher who does not blind himself to social and political problems, but gazes on them calmly, knowing them to be only just a little more concrete than mists or rising water.

About 1680 *famille verte* comes into its full strength. Every imaginable colour is now used, and the stories in which the Chinese are steeped and which had been written down in Sung times (960–1279) now begin to appear on porcelain, causing many varieties of design. Through some of these designs we can study the life of China for hundreds of years past, with all its social customs and history. Emperors, statesmen, scholars and warriors are all depicted. The warriors, it is true, look more like jugglers than fighters, for they often have balls which they throw at their opponents instead of spears. Chinese literature is also represented, with scenes from famous plays and romances, painted in the most brilliant colours with predominating bright greens and reds.

In *Chinese Porcelain* W. G. Gulland refers to a magnificent 'vase of farewell' of the K'ang Hsi period, decorated in various greens with a

48

good deal of aubergine, and also yellow, red and black, sparingly used. The design is probably taken from the poem by Wang Wei (A.D. 699–759) who was one of the foremost poets of the T'ang dynasty. His lines in bidding adieu to Mêng Hao-jan when the latter was seeking refuge on the mountains are well known, and a variation on them is to be found in Mahler's *Der Abschied* in his *Lied von Der Erde* (Song of the Earth):

> Dismounted, o'er wine
> We had said our last say;
> Then I whispered, 'Dear friend,
> Tell me, whither away?'
> 'Alas!' he replied,
> 'I am sick of life's ills,
> And I long for repose
> On slumbering hills.
> But oh, seek not to pierce
> Where my footsteps may stray,
> The white clouds will soothe me
> For ever and ay. . . .

On some bowls we find designs taken from an Imperial album of ploughing and weaving, which tell us how these beautiful objects were used to encourage the labourers in their growing of rice and silk-making. There are, however, many pieces ornamented much more simply, such as some magnificent vases and dishes with elaborate decoration, that is to say, scattered flowers on a soft green dotted ground, enlivened by red. As nature abhors a vacuum, so the Chinese usually abhorred blank undecorated spaces in their designs. There are numerous intricate designs used profusely in the decoration of porcelain. These are often of a conventional and symbolic type, being arabesque or *diaper patterns* arranged in rows or borders and employed as ornamental panels. The simplest is the *meander* or *key pattern*. The Chinese called it the 'thunder pattern', because it represented clouds and thunder. Yetts, in *Symbolism in Chinese Art*, tell us: 'Rain was essential to their very existence, and the

49

Famille verte Saucer-dish. Diameter: 13½ ins. K'ang Hsi period.

symbol for thunder typified the downpour that brought the heaven-sent gift of abundance.' The 'swastika', with its crampons that the Nazis have reversed, was another element of decoration, whilst other designs included trellis-work, which sometimes appears as a band or border; diamond-work, either plain or flowered; scroll-work, largely employed in the decoration of the later pieces of porcelain, as is curl-work; fish-roe, found in both early and late china-ware, and octagons and squares, to be seen mostly on egg-shell plates.

Flowers of the *famille verte* are usually prunus, peony, lotus, chrysanthemum and almond. The plum (or prunus) represents winter, the peony, spring, the lotus, summer, and the chrysanthemum, autumn. The lotus was a very common Buddhist symbol. In K'ang Hsi's reign we even find teapots shaped like lotus leaves: an example is to be found in the British Museum. To the Chinese, the lotus is a symbol of purity and perfection because it grows out of mud and is not defiled. Anesaki, in *Buddhist Art*, writes that Buddha himself saw his fellow-beings 'like lotus stems and buds on a lake, some immersed in the mud, others coming out of it and still others beginning to blossom. He determined to bring them all to full bloom and the bearing of fruit'.

Sometimes animals are depicted, such as horses, lions, storks, cranes, phoenixes, small birds, crabs and, of course, dragons. Père D'Entrecolles tells us: 'The Chinese are particularly successful in their grotesque and animals. I have seen a cat painted to the life, in the head of which a lamp was put which shone through the cat's two eyes and at night, the rats were terrified of it.' A humorous touch has been added to two tureens in the shape of ducks, now to be seen at Polesden Lacey. The potters have added a pigtail to the back of their necks, as every Chinaman was supposed to wear a pigtail out of reverence to the Emperor.

There were also beautiful cages for the keeping of choice specimens of butterflies, which were emblems of conjugal felicity. Very often one finds a particular flower or plant drawn with a particular bird. Thus the long-tail birds, phoenix, peacock, fowl and pheasant pair with the peony; the duck with the lotus; the swallow with the willow; the stork with the pine, as a symbol of longevity, etc.

In the *famille verte* figures, the tall, slender lady, known as the *Long Eliza*, is perhaps taller than the average Chinese woman. Could it be that the Chinese painters wanted their ladies to appear taller than they were in reality, so that the westerners, having never seen them in the flesh, would have a glamorized conception of their elegance?

Though *famille verte* reached the height of its glory in the reign of K'ang Hsi, more delicate versions of its colours appeared for over a century after his reign. Examples of these are bowls, dishes and vases, decorated with dragons, flowers, peonies and pomegranates, often outlined in black and washed in with bright colours. A good proportion of these are obtainable today.

Already in the last years of K'ang Hsi's reign, we find a delicacy of treatment unknown to its zenith. Paintings in miniature began to appear with delicate colouring, precise designs, and much careful attention to detail. K'ang Hsi's sixtieth birthday in 1713 was marked by the novelty of some delicate birthday plates and dishes, painted in *famille verte* on egg-shell, that is, very thin, almost transparent porcelain, with the inscription: 'A myriad longevities without ending'.

In the Percival David Foundation we find two dishes of this birthday service type, each decorated with a bird on a pendant fruiting bough. Some other pieces of the same period in the Foundation are decorated with a central motif, containing the character *Shou* (longevity); and some bear symbols of long life, such as the stork. There is also a very rare plate with ducks and aquatic plants on a river scene, and on another piece figures the Three Star God of happiness, rank and longevity.

K'ang Hsi's longevities and those of the *famille verte*, however, were soon to end, for a few years later, after the Emperor's death in 1722, saw the rise of the *famille rose* which was to eclipse the *famille verte* in popularity – rather ungratefully, since it owed its origins to none other than this same *famille verte*.

52

Famille Rose

In Leyden, about the year 1650, a Dutch chemist, Andreas Cassius, was at work on a discovery which was to prove invaluable to Chinese porcelain. From gold chloride and tin, he produced the rose-purple colour, named after him, 'purple of Cassius'.

Ever since the Ming dynasty the Chinese potters had had many colours at their disposal. Now they were to have the one colour that had, so far, eluded them: a rose-tint whose soft and delicate shade was to vary in their skilful hands from the palest of pinks to purple, including a much prized ruby hue.

Having for centuries prided themselves upon inventing their own colours, it must have seemed strange to them to have to rely, for once, upon a 'foreign devil' to give them this pink, which was to prove of all their colours the most popular. The exciting new tint, which before had been out of their reach, they named 'foreign colours'.

The Nuremberg enamellers were probably the first to take advantage of this, about the year 1680; but the Chinese painters did not allow more than half a century to pass before they had introduced it into their own palette, towards the end of the reign of K'ang Hsi.

It is a pleasing thought that K'ang Hsi, that great patron of the arts, just caught a glimpse of this *famille rose* before his death in 1722, for W. B. Honey tells us that one specimen of the early *famille rose* bears a date somewhere about 1721. This saucer dish, with a slight painting of peony sprays, is in the British Museum. Such specimens, however, are rare, and the *famille rose* did not come into its full glory until the reign of Yung

53

Famille rose bowl, white with floral decoration.
Diameter: 11 ins. Height: 5 ins. Ch'ien Lung period.

Cheng (1723–35). By the beginning of this period the *famille rose* palette, the 'Yang ts'ai', or 'foreign colours' of the Chinese had almost replaced *famille verte* in popularity, except on the cheapest of export ware. The new colours, including rose-pink and crimson, were chiefly opaque, and an opaque white also, was freely used, which permitted the blending of colours never seen before.

To the Chinese potters this 'foreign colours' seemed magical, for the pink would change colour in the kiln according to the temperature at which it was baked, turning from the palest of pinks to the deepest of

54

rose. Though not magic in their idea of the word, the Chinese painters certainly made a magical use of this colour, perhaps because they had the sense to use it sparingly, aiming at what for them was the perfect balance between the white paste of the background and the coloured decoration. To the Chinese eye the objects made for export were over-decorated. Therefore their *famille rose* falls into two styles: the Imperial and other wares intended for Chinese taste and those destined for export.

W. B. Honey tells us that the wares sent from the Imperial Palace to the London Exhibition of 1935 came 'as a minor revelation'. He describes them thus:

Unlaboured miniature painting in designs of great simplicity, giving full value to a beautiful white porcelain ground. . . . Sprays and flowering branches thrown across the surface of plates and vases, with intended lack of symmetry. . . . Birds painted with delicate naturalism. . . . Large dishes with flowering and fruiting peach sprays, from the Summer Palace at Peking. . . .

Unfortunately, these 'rarities' are seldom to be found outside museums today; but there are some splendid examples of them in the Percival David Foundation in London, as well as in the Victoria and Albert and the British Museums.

Those wares destined for export were often influenced by European designs, which the Chinese copied, sometimes with amusing inaccuracies. In the Victoria and Albert Museum there is a late eighteenth century bowl, decorated with the Chinese idea of an English hunt. The fox at the bottom of the bowl looks rather like a curious fish, while the ethereal-looking hounds around the side resemble minnows, and the riders in pastel-shaded coats, cracking whips, might have come straight out of an eighteenth century operetta.

Farmyard features and farm animals appear to have held an almost Beatrix Potter like place in Chinese affections. The Emperor Ch'ien Lung (1736–95), who wrote no less than 30 000 poems, gives a picture of this in a poem translated by Bushell:

> The hen and chickens close together
> With the cock in all his glory,
> With glowing tail, iron spurs,
> His head held straight erect
> In angry poise, ready for combat. . . .

The farm animals are very often mixed with flowers; the cock and peony seems to have been a favourite motif. A Chinese writer tells us:

These two are mentioned in the earliest of Chinese records: cocks to crow the morn, and even in the coffin we invariably put a cock's feather, so as to wake up the dead early to push on his journey to the underneath world. Peonies have been the subject of many ancient poems, and are considered the grandest of flowers, and moreover, true natives of China.

In the Percival David Foundation there is a delightful set of twelve cups and saucers of the Ch'ien Lung period, with cocks and peonies so gay that they look as if they had been made to decorate the Easter table. They are of fine white egg-shell porcelain, decorated in *famille rose* enamels, with a rooster standing on a rock beside a clump of peonies. Some plates of this period are even more profusely decorated. J. Lloyd Hyde, in *Chinese Porcelain for the European Market*, writes: 'Some plates are so elaborate that they seem almost not to have belonged to services, but to have been meant for wall-decoration.'

The Chinese love of flowers is well known. A saying of Confucius goes: 'If you have two loaves of bread, sell one and buy a flower.' Now Andreas Cassius's discovery, their 'foreign colours', enabled them to give full expression to their feeling for flowers in their decoration. 'Flowering branches run from the outside of the plate to the inside of the plate,' writes du Boulay in *Chinese Porcelain*, and Emil Hanover says of *famille rose*: 'It has a festive splendour compared with which European porcelain seems poor and lifeless.'

Perhaps it is only natural that *rose verte* was the first use to which these 'foreign colours' were put, in the Yung Cheng period (1723–35). At the beginning it is difficult to find a piece of *famille rose* without some trace of green in its decoration. The *rose verte* here looks very much like the *famille verte*, the only difference between the two being the introduction of pink, either in place of, or with the old iron-red.

> Pink and green,
> Fit for a Queen.

Thus goes the old rhyme, and pink and green, such as flowers with leaves, do blend beautifully together, one setting off the freshness of the other. The designs in *rose verte* are bolder than in the other types of *famille rose* and often bear a likeness to *famille verte* scenes.

No porcelain, however, shows greater variety of decoration than the *famille rose*. From the vigorously drawn *rose verte* it ranges to the miniature painting found on egg-shell dishes and plates, through the enamelled rose, where the white porcelain is hidden entirely by the painting. The *famille rose* palette was easier to manage than that of the *famille verte*, which enabled the painters to use a more meticulous style of decoration.

A great deal of the decoration of export porcelain was done at Canton, although the porcelain itself was made at Ching-tê-chên. This Canton-painted porcelain, at its best, was of egg-shell thinness, and when coloured on the back with ruby or pink was known as 'ruby-back'. A popular decoration on ruby-backed plates were children playing with rabbits and other animals.

Most of this porcelain was made in the eighteenth century, when the influence of European design had begun to make itself strongly felt. A good example is to be found in the Percival David Foundation. Painted on fine white porcelain with chicken-skin glaze in pale *famille rose* enamels is the figure of a shepherdess in Chinese dress, but with something of a European air about her. Around her are two very European-looking rams and three sheep, in a landscape of rocks and rushes. This vase is of the Ch'ien Lung period. The mingling of oriental and Western

Famille rose Vase, enamelled in
colours, with figures performing befor[e]
officials on terraces. Height: 18½ ins.
Nineteenth century.

Famille rose Punch bowl. Diameter: 14½ ins. Nineteenth century.

design is well illustrated by plates decorated with Chinese family scenes as centrepiece, and borders with designs imitating European ceramics. A valuable plate of this kind is sometimes to be found in London.

In Ch'ien Lung's reign, some animals changed character. Birds became more popular than dragons; also we are led to believe that the tiny, red squirrels, often to be found in the designs, may have been masquerading as foxes. The fox was sometimes looked upon as an animal of ill-omen. According to Couling in the *Encyclopaedia Sinica* under *Fairy Foxes*, demons would appear in the form of something like a fox. Possibly the designers were also influenced by a convert to Christianity who wished to illustrate the words: 'The little foxes who spoil the vines . . .'. It is certain that foxes were believed to be able to assume human shape, as a man or a beautiful girl, luring the unwary to ruin; but if bribed by offerings, they could also bestow wealth.

There is one sort of ware in *famille rose* which is neither in Chinese taste nor specially made to European design. This is the so-called *Batavian ware*, with coffee-brown ground and bold *famille rose* panels, which takes its name from the Dutch trading centre in Java.

Owing to its immense popularity, there were greater quantities of *famille rose* than of any other export porcelain sent from China to Europe, and fortunately a great deal of it is still obtainable today.

The objects made included tea, coffee and chocolate sets. It is worth noting that when a teacup has a handle it is probably not more than a hundred and fifty years old or so, for handles were not in use on teacups in Europe until the end of the eighteenth century. That is why people spoke of a 'dish of tea'. There were bowls of all sizes, from cups to eight-gallon punch-bowls. Some bowls for brides had designs of twin-fish, symbols of a happy marriage. Decorative plates sometimes had a good-wish mark on the reverse side, saying: 'Riches, honour and a prolonged spring' – spring, here, means prolonged youth.

Vases varied from the immense, sometimes known as 'Grenadier Vases', because Augustus the Strong was supposed to have exchanged a number of Grenadiers for such vases, to the tiny vases for flowers. Urns could also be giant-size. Père D'Entrecolles describes them as 'urns above three feet high, with lids which rose like a pyramid, a foot high'. There were models of porcelain animals, some of them in the form of tureens, such as the Swan in the Victoria and Albert Museum. There were also, though these are more rare, human figures. Candlesticks were made in great quantities, as were bedroom utensils, bottles, boxes, snuff-boxes, incense-burners and jars for *pot-pourri*. For the table there were salt-cellars and sweetmeat dishes, for the boudoir, decorative plaques and clock-cases.

Unfortunately, for the collector of *famille rose* there may be some startling pitfalls. Though a piece of *famille rose* is so easy to recognize that it instantly catches the eye, the novice is liable to make mistakes as to the dating of the respective pieces, since large numbers of such pieces have continued to be produced well into the late nineteenth century, and are copied even in the present day.

So be careful when you are looking for your 'magic bargains'.

Famille Noire and Famille Jaune

Unattainable goals

To complete our 'families' we must just touch on the *famille noire* and the *famille jaune*, that is to say, polychrome painting on black and yellow grounds, in the early part of the reign of K'ang Hsi. These pieces are usually only to be found in museums or private collections today. The chief pieces consist of vases of various shapes, covered with black which, when looked into closely, has a slight coating of green over the black. These vases are often decorated with white prunus blossom (hawthorn pattern) which stands out strikingly against the black background. A good example is to be seen in the Victoria and Albert Museum: a vase of rectangular shape decorated with prunus blossom, and a canary-coloured bird with green wings. Sometimes the white prunus blossom was mixed with flowers of other colours.

The large vases with green, black and yellow grounds (in which case they were sometimes known as the *famille jaune*) are of noble stature. Looking at them one can understand the Chinese idea that they were inspired by the curve of the female form. Apart from the flowers, boldly but sensitively painted, there are dragon designs, the dragon sometimes representing the Emperor, sometimes power; and also landscapes with birds on rocks.

Some vases, including jars and bottles, were covered with a mere black glaze, without the coating of green over it. They were decorated with coloured flowers or other designs, and are a 'plain' relation of the grander pieces which, still occasionally to be found, fetch very large prices today.

Armorial Porcelain

Noblesse oblige

If you were living in Europe during the eighteenth century, when K'ang Hsi was reigning in China, and you wished to give a wedding present to, say, your son, you would probably send your coat-of-arms all the way out to China to have it emblazoned on a dinner-service. But when you unpacked it on its return, you might, to your consternation, find that the attractive colour scheme of red, blue and green that you had envisaged was non-existent – instead your plates were returned with the words, 'Red, Blue and Green' painted on them. Never mind. This was the kind of risk you had to take if you wished to follow the fashion amongst the smart families of Europe. And it might have been much worse. For instance, one unfortunate family sent out their motto 'Think and Thank' and it came back to them 'Stink and Stank', simply because the Chinese used to set down words as they appeared to them, without thinking of their meaning.

In spite of the risks incurred the noble families of Europe continued to order this Chinese *armorial porcelain*. These Arms were the earliest designs sent from Europe to be copied in China and, in London, had often been sketched in colour and painted by members of the College of Heralds. The fashion began about 1700 and continued until almost 1820, when the European factories, such as Worcester, began to produce good armorial china of their own.

Why did European families send their Arms so far away to be copied? One can only imagine that they may have been influenced by the Chinese cult of ancestor-worship or maybe, the Chinese themselves, with their respect for the family, fancied that this was an excellent way of pleasing their European customers. Anyway, they were inclined to embellish the coats-of-arms and crests with decorations of their own, which gave to the stately family china an exotic oriental look. Sometimes, too, the heraldic beasts designed by the Chinese were apt to lead to disappointment. Imagine unpacking a set with the crest of the lion which you as a family had always been proud of, to find that it had turned into a tiger!

In the beginning years, 1700–23, the shields were in early English or Jacobean style. The designs were often in underglaze blue, with the arms in colour. They had green borders and flowers on the back. From 1735–55 the Arms changed from Jacobean to Rococo, with curves and shells. Pink designs also appeared. The decoration included birds, buildings and shipping scenes as well as copies of French prints, fox-hunts and flower paintings.

The last years of the century saw the arms enclosed in spade-shaped shields with flowers and still later, towards the beginning of the nine-teenth century there were borders in deep blue. Some of the old bills for these services have been carefully preserved by the families concerned.

For students of heraldry this *armorial porcelain* has a special interest, for although most of the pieces are undated, the heraldic design itself can sometimes supply an approximate date. Some collectors even buy whole services of *armorial porcelain*, keeping a few choice specimens for them-selves and then generously advertising the remaining pieces in the hopes that they may fall into the hands of their original families. So, if a family today are searching, as their ancestors did, for a wedding present in porcelain, it is a possibility that they might even find part of a service with their own coat-of-arms or, at any rate, the coat-of-arms of a near relative.

The position in America was somewhat different from that in Europe, for the *armorial porcelain* which the Americans began to order immedi-ately after the War of Independence, can be divided into two categories.

The first belonged to families who already possessed coats-of-arms and the second was the pseudo-armorial where, in default of a coat-of-arms, the initials of the family were usually printed in gilt within a gilt-trimmed shield.

An example of the first type was that of Colonel Richard Lees, one of the first settlers in Virginia, who had a right to the Arms of the Lees of Shropshire in England; whereas an interesting illustration of the second type is to be found in an order given by a prominent USA citizen, William Reed, for a dinner-service of four hundred pieces with the initial 'R' in a gilt cipher. Another early American order came from John Stark of New Hampshire, who wished to have his initials and two shields, one on each side of every piece; but the more modest Clintons were content to choose designs of a platter and basin with the words: 'For Us, Man and Wife'. Isaac and Mary Morris, self-effacing couple that they must have been, simply had inscribed: 'A Farmer and His Cow'. A strong-minded lady, however, Deborah Fairfax Anderson, was less modest. She had her initials 'D. F. A.' inscribed underneath a design of Minerva and Cupid.

So anxious were the Americans to celebrate their new found sense of independence that their ships were waiting in American harbours, ready to set sail for China the minute that peace had been declared. The Chinese received their new clients with enthusiasm, but could not resist calling them 'Flowery Flag Devils', instead of the 'Foreign Devils', which was their nickname for the Europeans. So English and American ships left Canton for the first time, their recent differences sunk in a common aim – that of carrying their precious cargoes safely homewards.

Monochromes

Looking as good as they sound

A collector, showing us an extremely early vase of a soft blue colour, told us that the Chinese would describe this as: 'Blue as the sky after rain'. To lovers of colour these all-over lustrous glazes, known as monochromes, delight the senses as much as the poetical descriptions of their hues.

One type of monochrome often to be seen today is known by the name of *celadon*. There are two theories as to the origin of this name. Some hold that it derived from 'Salah-ed-din', a Sultan of Egypt, who sent forty pieces of this green-ware to Nur-ed-din, a Sultan of Damascus in 1171. A more modern opinion suggests that it was named after a character called *Céladon* who wore a green costume in a seventeenth century French romance, entitled *L'Astrée*. However this may be, the colour probably originated from the desire of the Chinese to imitate their favourite jade-stone in all its shades, from a dark-green to a milky-white, including 'sea-green', 'cucumber-green', 'camelia-leaf green', etc.

Some of these specimens in the form of cups were sent by the Sultan of Egypt to Lorenzo de Medici in 1487. Such cups were much treasured as they were supposed to change colour if any poisonous substance were put into them.

There are, however, many variations of monochrome colours. In the Ming period, during the reign of Hsüan Te (1426–35), the potters specialized in 'sacrificial red' or 'precious stone red', so-called because rubies or other stones were supposed to be used in its preparation. On the whole the most famous fifteenth century coloured glazes are the cobalt-blues and copper-reds. Though collectors may have to search

65

diligently for Ming monochromes, they are still available, at a price.

The Ch'ing period was later to copy many of these colours of the Ming. A particularly lovely purplish-violet tone was known as 'Temple of Heaven' blue, because the colour was taken from the tiles and altar vessels of a Peking temple itself. A sharp contrast in colour are the lustrous black monochromes, 'mirror-black', discovered during the K'ang Hsi period. This period also revived the turquoise glazes, known to the Chinese as 'Kingfisher-blue' or 'peacock-green', which had been made in China as early as the fifteenth century. Also outstanding are the Imperial yellow glazes, the rare ones with designs of dragons, often a symbol of the Emperor, on them. An amusing invention for a lady of class were the yellow water-buffaloes, made for pillows, so that she could rest her head upon them without spoiling her hair-do.

Some of these monochromes had a 'crackled glaze', originally an error in the kilns, but afterwards produced deliberately. The Chinese could turn out crackle of any size. When this was small crackle, it was called by the French '*truité*', because it looked like the scales of a trout.

Another so-called 'error' that turned out to be a stroke of good fortune were the famous '*flambé glazes*'. These were discovered in the later Ming period, during an attempt to produce the underglaze copper-red of the earlier Ming. When the coloured glaze was applied to the paste, it was often exposed to the extreme heat of the first firing. This sometimes caused the glaze to change colour and to take on variegated hues, which the French called '*flambé*' and the English 'splashed'. The Chinese were so delighted with these freak results that they soon learnt to produce them at will. In the Ch'ing period, during the reign of K'ang Hsi, this *flambé* art was very much taken up and developed. Some attractive glazes in which the copper-red, treated in this way, produced pale red and brownish colours were known as 'peach-bloom', 'apple-red' and 'bean-red'. There were reds streaked with grey, purple, lavender and opalescent blue. A popular K'ang Hsi red was known as *sang de bœuf* (ox-blood), so-called because of its deep blood-red colour.

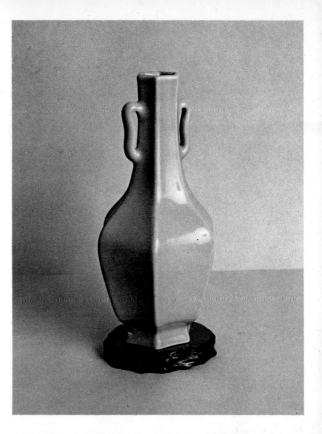

Celadon Monochrome Vase.
Height: 10½ ins. Eighteenth century.

Monochrome Bowl, mules liver.
Diameter: 8 ins. Ch'ien Lung period.

Brush-pot, apple-green, with design of dragon and carp.
Height: 5½ ins. Circa 1821.

There is an amusing, if doubtful, story about how *sang de bœuf* was first discovered. The Emperor had ordered some precious grccn vases to be made for his personal use. The potters put them in the kilns, then went off to a party and got drunk, forgetting all about their work. When they eventually returned and opened up the kilns, they found, to their horror, that the precious vases had turned to a brilliant red. Terrified of the Emperor's wrath, they fled the country. Meanwhile, the Emperor, impatient for his vases, went down to inspect the kilns personally, and there stood these glorious red vases! By overheating they had turned into *sang de bœuf*. The enthusiastic Emperor organized a search for the potters, who were eventually found hiding in a pigsty. What must have been their astonishment when they were brought back to the Emperor, who rewarded them handsomely for their brilliant new invention! *Sang de bœuf* reds of very fine colours were used in the nineteenth century on the typical heavy-footed vases of the period.

Another variation, in the Ch'ing period, was the so-called *soufflé* decoration. Jacquemart tells us how Père D'Entrecolles describes this process:

The colour made of the proper consistency is placed in a tube, one end of which is covered with a close gauze; by blowing through the other end little drops filled with air are precipitated upon the enamel. These burst when coming in contact with the sides of the piece and reduce themselves into little contiguous circles, forming a net-work of the finest lace. Sometimes the soufflé colour is blue, more often of a carmine red, which at first sight, gives to the piece the appearance of a violet-like enamel. This decoration often fails, the little drops do not burst, but form, on the contrary, into little veins which run half-melted into the starch-blue glazes. Hence results a peculiar decoration very agreeable to the eye: *jasper*, not less sought after than the soufflé itself.

Soufflé-blue is known also as 'powder-blue', which the French call *bleu fouetté*. It has a speckled appearance, owing to the colour being put on unevenly. The blue under the glaze sometimes extends over the whole surface, but often white panels are left which are decorated with figures, flowers and symbols in blue and red under the glaze in *famille verte* style. We found a particularly attractive powder-blue vase, which was decorated over the blue glaze with red and silver fish. It was of the K'ang Hsi period.

The great variety of shape and brilliance of colour of these 'crackled', 'flambé', 'celadon' and other coloured monochromes makes them look at their best when set off and framed in a form of bronze, once called by the French 'Ormolu', but now known as 'bronzed ore'. Monochromes mounted in this manner are more often to be seen in French collections than in English ones.

Some of these monochromes have an intriguing kind of decoration, known as 'secret'. This began in Ming times. The design was lightly incised into the body before glazing, and could only be seen, like a water-mark, when the object was held up to the light. Others were decorated with raised ornaments, usually with figures, flowers or leaves.

One way of telling whether a monochrome, especially a *sang de bœuf*, is good quality and has a fair chance of being eighteenth century, is to examine its base or foot. If one feels round the base, it should be perfectly smooth to the touch. If, on the contrary, it is chipped or gritty or rough to the touch, it is likely to be a later production.

With all the wealth of imagination and skill put into their colouring and their shape, these fine monochromes stand out proudly, looking as good as their names.

Vase, kingfisher-blue, with dragon curled round.
Height: 13½ ins. Late nineteenth century.

Blanc de Chine

Frozen in motion

Collectors may still make merry,
With their families, rose and green,
Pure beauty lies in the very
Heart of the blanc de chine.

Whites, viveous, candid, showy
Pearly and cream, we've seen;
These are but 'posé' and showy
On the shelf near our blanc de chine.

Some may consider the writer of this poem a little over-enthusiastic but it is true that in the finest of these pieces the potters have caught and held a beauty that can satisfy the greatest purist in taste. *Blanc de chine*, as the French lovingly named it, can be compared to ivory; and it is possible that in the early days of its invention the Chinese were trying to imitate ivory in porcelain, in the same way as they imitated jade.

When did *blanc de chine* first make an appearance? None of the authorities seems to be quite sure, but it is generally thought that it might have been about the beginning of the seventeenth century, in the Ming dynasty. Anyhow, it was not made at Ching-tê-chên, but at Te-hua, in the province of Fukien.

Unlike the Imperial wares which were subsidized, *blanc de chine* had to make its own way commercially, and that is why we find numerous small wares, such as censers, home-altars and objects for domestic use which were destined for the humblest home. It was the custom to burn incense on a home-altar when visitors appeared, although some of the larger censers were often put to the use of holding eggs and fruit and the tiny ones for storing trinkets and buttons. Some of these censers have found their way to the West and are obtainable today.

Like jade, *blanc de chine* has many gradations in colour, from a dead white to a creamy or greyish one – in fact, two pieces placed side by side are often seen to be of quite a different shade.

The figures of the Ming *blanc de chine* are modelled superbly and, with their shapes under their graceful drapery, seem really to be 'frozen in motion', to quote W. B. Honey. Character in face and figure is wonderfully portrayed, as in the frequently modelled Goddess of Mercy, who has a grace and serenity that is almost Madonna-like. Sometimes the tightly-curled hair of the Goddess looks appropriately like a judge's wig.

The *blanc de chine* made in the Ch'ing dynasty carried on the reputation which had been given it under the Ming, and the purity of its glass became the admiration of the West. No wonder, therefore, that the Chinese began to make figures in European style, such as Europeans armed with weapons for the chase, hounds on leashes, and road-travellers. These figures can often be dated by their costume. They also made toy-whistles, on which they caricatured Europeans, fabulous beasts, lions, tigers and camels.

Animals, as a whole, made good subjects for *blanc de chine* modelling. The Chinese eighteenth century Buddhist lions are naturalistic and their manes are carefully parted down the back, with tails extravagantly tufted and paws raised in the air. Some of the Buddhist lions, in pairs, have tubes to hold incense sticks, as do some birds. Larger animals included water-buffaloes, deer, elephants and horses, as well as dragons with their young. Cats were also represented, gazing musingly into the distance with that faraway innocent look, as if they could not possibly be guilty of attracting the poverty of which they were accused by Chinese belief.

Often choice specimens of *blanc de chine* cups, with included poems or

Blanc de chine Figure with Child. Height: 9½ ins. Eighteenth century.

literary inscriptions, would be kept in lined boxes by connoisseurs and taken out from time to time to be admired, then carefully put back again.

There were, however, many wares made for ordinary use, apart from the censers already mentioned. These include cups, bowls, dishes and vases, mostly decorated with animals and flowers in relief, such as lotus leaves, plum branches and, very occasionally, peonies. Fukien, like the rest of China, was famed for the beauty of its flowers, and the peony being rich in colour and petals, was often taken as the symbol of the rich and happy man. Lin Yutang in his book, *The Importance of Living*, tells us an interesting anecdote about this flower:

The Empress Wu of the T'ang dynasty commanded one day, in one of her megalomaniac whims, that all the flowers in the Imperial garden should bloom on a certain day in midwinter, just because she wanted it. The peony was the only one that dared to offend her Imperial Majesty by blooming a few hours late, and consequently all the thousands of pots of peony flowers were banished by Imperial decree from Sian, the capital, to Loyang.

Loyang, nothing daunted, continued to cultivate the peony, which flourished, and, as we see, became so popular that it is even modelled in relief in *blanc de chine*.

The *blanc de chine* cups, whether they had peony designs or not, do not seem to have been popular for tea-drinking, according to a Chinese writer, who tells us:

I use it (the cup) for tea and the tea is dull and colourless. I scold the boy, blaming his negligence, and ask someone else to do it, but the colour remains the same. If you put tea in a Ching-tê-chên cup it turns green. I tried it and it is true. That is why the porcelain of Te-hua (*blanc de chine*) is unpopular for tea-drinking.

Some of these cups may not have been easy to drink out of, especially if they were in the favourite form of a rhinoceros horn, or even the Chinese trick-cup which played jokes on the would-be drinker. But for fine tea-drinking by poets and scholars, there were cups shaped like magnolia leaves, in which one can only imagine that the tea tasted good. There were also graceful tea and coffee-pots, ewers, mugs and porringers – in fact, crockery to suit all tastes to put 'on the shelf (with) our *blanc de chine*.

Canton Enamels on Metal

For my lady's chamber

A Chinese writer of the eighteenth century, Wen Fang-su, tells us in words to this effect: 'They (Canton enamels) are only fit for use as ornaments of ladies' apartments, not at all for the chaste furniture of the library of a scholar.'

The Chinese, it seems, were inclined to look upon their Canton enamel work as a poor relation of their splendid porcelain, not fit for a scholar or indeed for any but those with a modest income, who could not afford to buy the more expensive porcelain. This may have been because the colours were painted on a metal base, on a ground of opaque enamel, usually white, and they sank into the background. They therefore had neither the freshness nor the beauty that the Chinese expected to find on their porcelain.

The craft was also somewhat 'foreign' to the Chinese, having been introduced into China by foreign missionaries, in the early years of the eighteenth century.

Although the Chinese seemed to look upon this ware with some suspicion, the Emperor K'ang Hsi evidently thought that the technique justified a place in his School of Arts, for in 1713 he set up a special workshop for its manufacture. Thus under his august patronage, the 'poor relation' took courage, and by the following reign of Yung Cheng in 1723, Canton enamel began to find its way to Europe. By the time of Ch'ien Lung's reign (1736–95) a finer form of Canton enamel was being made in the pure Chinese taste, including landscape panels for the Imperial Court, about which the Emperor Ch'ien Lung thought highly enough to write some of his poems.

Though it has not the brilliance of porcelain, the colours being softer, Canton enamel still has a great attraction for the home. Being enamelled on a metal base, it does not break as easily as porcelain, and its designs, usually floral, have a certain charm of their own on objects such as small teapots, ashtrays, incense-burners, vases, etc.

Today, many wares are to be found at advantageous prices that 'My Lady' would be pleased to put in her 'Chamber'.

The Bronzes

Chimes through the ages

It is an interesting thought that many of the shapes and subjects we so much admire on Chinese ceramics were copied by the potters from one of the most ancient of art forms, that of fashioning bronzes, which had already begun in the Shang-Yin dynasty (1766–1122 B.C.). So long ago! Yet only recently a collector showed us a curious object which was probably one of the earliest forms of bell, but whose sound could only be heard by holding it upright before striking it.

It was difficult to believe that she had discovered this bell, for which she had paid only a few pounds, in a shop of mixed antiques, and she was thrilled when she learnt from the British Museum that its date was 500 B.C. Encouraged by her find, she began to hunt about through various shops, and was astonished to unearth a god of war in lacquered bronze of the Ming period, and a Bodhisattva, an aspiring Buddha. Nor did her search end there. She now has a large and beautiful incense-burner in bronze, belonging to the Ch'ien Lung period, as well as another curious censer from the same period reminiscent of the *Hands* sculpted by Rodin, a bronze kylin (Ch'i-lin) with its hair blowing in the wind and many other curious and interesting bronze objects. How did she come by all this? No book pointed the way, for any she had read stopped short just after the beginning of A.D., leading her to believe that these bronzes, interesting though they might be, were a curious relic of the past to be seen in museums, but completely unobtainable nowadays.

She came to the conclusion that this very lack of pointers in books and magazines on antiques had made these bronzes strangely available.

Bronze Dogs of Fo.
Early nineteenth century.

Chinese incense burner in
bronze. Represents
Buddha's fingers. 12 ins.
long. Ch'ien Lung period.

Chinese 'Ting' form of cauldron, decorated with low archaic relief. Height: 5 ins. Diameter: 5½ ins. Circa 500 B.C.

Four-legged Chinese Cauldron in archaic style, bronze with gold and silver inlay and traces of malacca patina. Stand with elephant heads. Height: 6½ ins. Probably Sung period.

Few people were looking for them, for few people knew that they existed, particularly in the Ming and Ch'ing periods. Her best hunting-ground was in mixed antique shops, for the dealers in these usually wish to get rid of objects that are not directly in their line, and very often among the period furniture in such shops there sits a bronze Buddha and, hiding behind a chest or a writing-table, a pot, a bronze mirror or a bell.

How fascinating to come upon one of these! These early bronzes owe their creation to the cult of ancestor-worship which, for the Chinese, was of the highest importance. This was not so much because they worshipped their ancestors as because they wished to keep on good terms with the dead, for these dead, it was believed, could make or mar family life. Properly respected and attended to, these ancestors could bring happiness, fertility and longevity. Nothing, therefore, could be too good for them. The most precious of metals known at that time was used, an alloy of copper and tin, and from this the craftsmen, as early as the Shang-Yin dynasty, brought forth some of the most beautiful examples of metal-work that the world has seen.

These bronzes were the forerunners of those T'ang horses and the whole world of underground tomb figures, considered necessary for the life hereafter.

The bronze workers did not give all their attention to ancestors, for the gods had also to be considered and their favours sought. How could this be better done than by using symbols on the ritual vessels which would tell the gods what human beings desired of them in the most reverent way that the craftsmen could invent? Thus wonderful decorations came into being. The decorators gave the very best of themselves, so that the designs they created transcended art into the realm of the spiritual. Their spirals and scrolls represent thunder, lightning and rain; their curious and rather terrifying animal masks are set in the midst of whirlpools resembling the waves of the sea. Their shells were either

ize T'ang Mirror (reverse side)
Diameter: 5 ins.

symbols of fertility or prayers for wealth, for under the Shangs a shell was used as a coin. The dragon, too, makes its first appearance in this dynasty. It is supposed to represent both heaven and earth, creating the harmony between the two which brings fertility. Later, as we have seen, it became the symbol of the Emperor, just as the pheasant, the emblem of the Sun, became the symbol of the Empress.

Other creatures used for these early bronzes were the cicada and the snake, supposed to represent the harvest and water; the owl, symbol of darkness and of the night, and the elephant which is again a symbol of fertility.

With the conquest of the country which led to the Chou dynasty (1122–221 B.C.), a change takes place. Decorations are now made purely for delight in their artistic effect. The craftsmen are no longer inspired by their feeling for religion. In the late Chou period the animals become less symbolic, more realistic, and human figures appear for the first time. The use of inlay, gold, silver and turquoise on stone and metal, is now introduced, and the metal once used for spiritual purposes enters the ladies' apartments in the form of bronze mirrors.

During the Han dynasty (206 B.C.–A.D. 220) these mirrors became more numerous. The utensils themselves became simpler, but decorations were still executed with the utmost skill and there was an attempt to bring movement into design.

Though the T'ang dynasty saw the great era of bronze drawing to a close, the later bronzes nevertheless catch some of the spirit of their grand heritage: the bronze bell, together with the other vessels, has rung down through the ages.

ze bell, mounted in carved wood. Ming period or earlier.
ht: 12 ins.

Jade

The Chinese have never accepted the judgement of the world as to the importance and value of so-called ' precious stones'. The great rubies so prized by the Indian Rajahs, the emeralds, the sapphires and the diamonds all took second place in their estimation compared with the most treasured of stones, jade. This stone had for them a religious and spiritual significance. Confucius writes: 'Its edges look sharp but they do not cut, like justice. It does not conceal flaws, like truthfulness.' And a Confucian scholar of the second century A.D., developing this idea, describes jade in this way:

It has five virtues. There is warmth in its lustre and brilliancy, this is the manner of kindness; its soft interior may be viewed from outside revealing (the goodness) within, this is the manner of rectitude; its note is tranquil and high and carries far and wide, this is the way of wisdom; it may be broken but cannot be twisted, this is the manner of bravery; its sharp edges are not intended for violence, this is the way of purity. . . .

And all this is summed up in an old Chinese book of poetry, which tells us: 'When I think of a wise man he reminds me of jade.' Another Chinese writer informs us: 'The superior man competes in virtue with jade.'

Jade (the Chinese name for it is '*Yu*') has its roots deep down in antiquity. It is made out of two separate minerals, nephrite and jadeite, both of these names being derived from parts of the human body: *jade*, from the Spanish '*Ijada*' meaning loins, and *nephrite* from the Greek '*νεφρός*', which means kidneys. The explanation of this is that this stone, taken in the form of powder, was believed to be a cure for diseases of the kidneys.

Neither nephrite nor jadeite was found inside China itself. Nephrite was found in Turkestan, Siberia, Alaska, Central America, New Zealand and Silesia, while jadeite came mostly from Burma.

Both stones have a great variety of colours, but nephrite's shades of green, varying from dark to light, are not as vivid as jadeite greens. Nevertheless this nephrite was supposed to have been attracted by femininity, for much of it is said to have been found by women wading in mountain-streams. It was believed that the naked femininity appealed to the masculine qualities said to be possessed by jade.

However this may be, these masculine qualities submitted themselves to the Shang craftsmen as early as 1766–1122(?) B.C., who mastered the technique of shaping and drilling jade, already fashioning handles, ceremonial blades, discs, tubes, pendants for adornment, arrowheads and animal figures. The decoration on this early jade was produced by raised or incised lines and already shows the beginnings of very fine craftsmanship.

The Chou dynasty (1122–221 B.C.) carried this craftsmanship further, carving the most complicated objects and achieving a standard of excellence which foreshadowed that of the eighteenth century, when the art of jade-carving had attained a new high standard.

During the Han dynasty (206 B.C.–A.D. 220) jade copies the tomb figures. As far back as this dynasty the Imperial Family used the horse and the bear carved in jade as omens for the duration of Imperial rule. It is said that the vision of a jade horse appeared every time that a noble and virtuous man ascended the throne.

It is not astonishing that jade, considered as a symbol of virtue, should be associated with Buddha. Buddhism was adopted in China around A.D. 67, and had a great influence upon jade carving. The lotus-flower, so often represented in carved jade was, as we have seen, a favourite symbol of the Buddha.

The T'ang dynasty (A.D. 618–906) produced articles for personal adornment, such as girdles, hair-ornaments and comb-backs, some of which have survived. The Chinese have always been noted for getting the utmost out of life by combining sensual and aesthetic pleasures. Thus the T'ang poet, Li-Po, a notorious wine-lover, speaks of 'fragrant amber wine served in cups of jade'. But much earlier than this, in the twelfth century B.C., there was a poem written, which is possibly the oldest drinking-song in the world:

> The dew is heavy on the grass.
> At last the sun is set.
> Fill up, fill up the cups of jade
> The night's before us yet!
>
> All night the dew will heavy lie
> Upon the grass and clover;
> Too soon, too soon, the dew will dry,
> Too soon the night be over.
>   (translation by HELEN WADDELL)

The Sung dynasty (A.D. 960–1279) innovated a 'cup of jade' in the form of a rhinoceros horn, and also made cylindrical cups. This dynasty was fond of making jade vases in the style of archaic bronze vases. One wonders if these were made to set off the arrangement of certain flowers, aesthetically so important to the Chinese. In *The Importance of Living*, Lin Yutang tells us: 'In putting flowers in . . . vases one should arrange them so that the size and height of the vase match with those of the flowers, while the shade and depth of its colour should contrast with them.' Certain it is that from the Sung dynasty onwards, flowers of all kinds were the subject of many jade carvings.

In the Yuan dynasty (A.D. 1280–1368) under the famous Emperor Kubla Khan, Marco Polo, the explorer and one of the first Europeans to reach the Court of the Son of Heaven, might well have dined off dishes of jade, though it seems that when he came home and told his

Jade in two shades of green, with birds on either side of bamboo trunk.
Nineteenth century.

Pale green Jade Stem-cup.
Height: 2½ ins. Eighteenth century.

'traveller's tale' his Venetian countrymen were sceptical. He would also have seen the carving in jade not only of flowers but of butterflies, dragonflies, grasshoppers, crickets and cicadas, as well as elephants and recumbent buffaloes. Jade carving in this Yuan period developed great subtlety, for in the carving of an insect on a leaf, the leaf was of one shade of green and the insect of another.

So we see that jade, sometimes called a 'stone that is beautiful', has a long heritage; and it is only natural that around it should grow many legends and superstitions. For instance, it played an essential part in religious ceremonies, one of its magic properties being that it was supposed to protect the corpse from the invasion of demons; and as it was believed to possess qualities of virtue, it was used as a charm against evil spirits, and also as a cure against disease. In some articles of adornment, such as thumb-rings, ear-rings, bracelets, hairpins and linked chains which were tokens of friendship, its virtue was thought to be conveyed to the wearer, so that it acted like a kind of mascot.

Bowl incised with Dragon in Clouds.

In the Ming dynasty (A.D. 1368–1644) jade returned to its heritage of the T'ang, and copied T'ang trifles, such as flutes, lutes and hairpins. The Ming period is renowned, also, for introducing that beautiful nephrite known as 'white jade' or 'mutton-fat jade' which the Emperors of China used on their sceptres. During this period jade was carved into landscapes, with small animals and recumbent horses in them. We have a good example of this in the National Trust House at Polesden Lacey, where in one of the cabinets, delicate horses can be seen carved into a mountain. In spite of this art of craftsmanship, Burling tells us in his book, *Chinese Art*, that:

A piece of jade would be kept and studied for months or even years, before a decision could be reached as to the best way to use it. One of the Ming Emperors acquired a rough piece of jade with green markings. He suggested to his most skilful carver that it be made into a piece showing a dragon fighting two Fo-Dogs. The sculptor took the piece in his hands, studied it thoughtfully, and replied: 'Your Majesty! Heaven has already shaped this piece of jade. It represents four carp swimming through green weeds in the lake of the Celestial Palace.' And so it was made.

We get the same idea from a poem by Michelangelo:

> The best of artists hath no thought to show
> Which the rough stone in its superfluous shell
> Doth not include; to break the marble spell
> Is all the hand that serves the brain can do.

But the brain was capable of discovering, and during the Ch'ing dynasty (A.D. 1644–1912), as we have seen, a great discovery was made: that of jadeite. To many, the eighteenth century Ch'ing is considered the finest period for jade. China's wealth and prosperity created an enormous demand for it, both from the Imperial House and the wealthy merchants. In the Victoria and Albert Museum, belonging to the Salting bequest, there is a curious eighteenth century jade vase in the form of pine and bamboo trunks with deer, crane and the sacred fungus, all of which stand for emblems of longevity. The deer, supposed by the Chinese to live to a great age, is the only animal which is able to find the sacred fungus of immortality, while the crane under a pine tree is a common emblem of longevity.

Another delightful jade object from a private collection is a bowl with a dragon in clouds incised on it. When held up to the light, we get the illusion that the dragon is coming out of the clouds.

But jade was not just for the rich, but for all people. Even the farmers wore little ornaments in the shape of ploughshares, and workmen wore them in the shape of axes, whilst married women sported pins and needles or jade ear-rings, hairpins and ornaments, bought for them by their husbands. There was scarcely a Chinese woman who did not own at least one piece of jade, the reason being that many small fragments were left over from the carving of the larger pieces, enabling numerous little objects to be sold cheaply.

The Emperor Ch'ien Lung, though ordering enormous carvings of mountains with streams, trees, pavilions and bamboo groves, peopled with literary scholars, had a foible for small objects in white jade; for instance, small brush rests shaped like mountain ranges.

Though there is a quantity of jade available today, to be found in sale rooms and some specialist shops, it is very difficult to give indications of price as these vary enormously with the quality. Objects of the rarest quality would certainly reach the thousands. Some of the carved ornaments sold as jade are made of a greenish white soapstone or even of opaque green glass. This is, however, easy to detect, for the glass shows air-bubbles, and soapstone being soft, leaves marks when scratched with a knife. True jade will never show such a mark when scratched, and is cold, smooth and hard to the touch.

This stone, as delightful to the touch as to the eye, is not merely a stone. To the Chinese it is the concentrated essence of hills and water. Thus Mayers in his *Chinese Reader's Manual* tell us:

In the language of alchemy . . . 'beverage of jade' was the name given to the supreme elixir which combines the virtues of the draught of immortality and the philosopher's stone.

Chinese Ivory

The elephant's generous excuse

'For ivory is a beautiful material; it is the elephant's generous excuse for his clumsiness and, at the same time, the sword-point of his strength.' Thus writes a poet about a material mentioned by a Chinese scholar as far back as 450 B.C. This scholar pities the elephant whose tusks will be used for ivory, which was of such value that it was accepted by the court in payment of taxes and tributes. Some two hundred years later a historian informs us that a certain minister tried to curry favour with his prince by giving him an ivory bed; and still later we are told that the rank of court officials could be distinguished by the different ivory tablets which they wore. But these precious tusks were also put to less solemn uses:

The courtesans dip their slender fingers in ivory boxes containing perfumed cosmetics; the gourmets carry with them their own little ivory sticks for eating rice and the new rich hang their hats on ivory hat-stands, while men of the world admire their favourite crickets through the delicate fretwork of ivory forming the lids of the special boxes carved out of gourds. I myself have bought a tiny bridge of ivory on which I rest my wrist while writing.

The most prized ivory objects were made from the tusks of elephants, transported, when the Chinese supply gave out, from Burma and India, and later from Africa. The tusks of other animals, such as the walrus and the hippopotamus, were also used, the quality of the ivory depending very much upon its growth, colour and brilliance.

In the early days only the Imperial families could afford such a precious material. Workshops founded by the court during the Sung dynasty (A.D. 960–1279) made small articles of ivory furnitures for the palace, as well as ornaments for personal use. Ivory, even more than jade, lent itself to carving, for the carver soon found that he could make the curves as soft as he wished. However, it is perhaps in the Ming dynasty that ivory, that 'beautiful material', was appreciated to the full, in texture, grain and colour. The Ming artists discovered ivory to be the ideal material for small statues. Such was the reverence of the Ming religious carvers for ivory that they left its form intact, considering it to be almost a revelation of the supernatural and so to be treated with awe. Sometimes the carver would see in the grain of his ivory the wrinkled skin of an old man, which he would try skilfully to bring out; sometimes the grace of a young girl would suggest itself to him through the curve of a tusk. But, apart from this, the Ming artist was an instinctive portraitist and, except when carving conventional figures such as the Buddha and the Eight Immortals, he would give free rein to his imagination, using living models for his human figures. Here the carver showed his reverence for old age, for he admitted that he preferred to carve elderly people because their faces had in them wisdom, tolerance, humour and resignation. The Chinese have always respected age. Writing in 1938, Lin Yutang tells us, in his book, *The Importance of Living*:

In China, the first question a person asks the other on an official call, after asking about his name or surname is: 'What is your glorious age?' If the person replies apologetically that he is twenty-three or twenty-eight, the other party generally comforts him by saying that he has still a glorious future, and that one day he may become old. But if the person replies that he is thirty-five or thirty-eight, the other party immediately exclaims with deep respect: 'Good luck!' Enthusiasm grows in proportion as the gentleman is able to report a higher and higher age, and if the person is anywhere over fifty, the inquirer immediately drops his voice in humility and respect.

The Ming carving had, however, its entertaining side. Usually the figures were clothed, but the exception was a small female figure made

93

Ivory Figure of one of th
Eight Immortals.
Height: 7½ ins. Ming per

specially for physicians. This was because a male doctor was not supposed to examine the body of a sick woman, so a little ivory figure was carried to the patient's bedside, who would put her hand through the bed curtains and indicate, on the figure, the exact spot where she felt the pain. Some of these little figures have come down to us today.

Many carvings date from the last years of the Ming dynasty, and a few were still being produced in the Ch'ing period. Such were the *pi-tongs*, round bowls carved out of the hollow roots of large tusks, in which the writer put his writing and painting brushes. The first *pi-tongs* were without decoration, but during the last years of the Ming period and the first of the Ch'ing, they were etched with garden scenes, landscapes and processions.

The Ch'ing dynasty went in for architectural models of houses, such as that to be seen in Hatfield House, Hertfordshire. This is an exquisite ivory model, with the Buddhist 'Dogs of Fo' guarding the entrance to the gate and figures standing on terraces at different levels. It is, of course, one of the models usually to be found inside a museum, but also at Hatfield House we can see a charming Chinese ivory casket with genre scenes of village life, such as people playing cards. Such caskets were made in quantities and some of them are obtainable today. An amusing innovation was the concentric balls, one inside the other (like those wooden Russian dolls, so popular nowadays), which were known as 'Devil's Work Balls'. Other objects included screens, lace-like fans, combs, hairpins, picture-frames, card-cases, bird-cages, cricket-cages, writing-brushes, paper-knives, umbrella-handles and cane-heads. There were also exquisite little models of various animals, elephants, lions, cows, bears, pigs and tiny rabbits with long ears. Placed together on a tray these look as if they had come out of a superior Noah's Ark.

It is a natural impulse to wish to touch ivory, and one can almost imagine that the warmth of many hands has gone into and enriched this 'beautiful material'.

Chinese Snuff-Bottles

The collector's fantasy

W. W. Winkworth, writing in the *Country Life Annual* about 1954, tells us: 'Collecting Chinese snuff-bottles is like making an indoor garden in miniature, and not too costly if one is prepared to do without the obviously precious materials.'

Some snuff-bottles were decked out proudly in gold and jade and these defy most collectors nowadays, but others were decorated with the more modest adornments of amber, ivory, horn, porcelain, glass, silver, pewter, onyx, rock crystal, lacquer, etc. The materials chosen were almost endless and the collector today would find himself in good company with the collector of the seventeenth century, for from the time when these fascinating little bottles first made their appearance, they were collected eagerly in all their various materials by members of the aristocracy, who did not confine themselves merely to gold and jade.

The Chinese and the Europeans started the habit of taking snuff at about the same time, around 1650, which was at the beginning of the Ch'ing dynasty in China. The Chinese snuff-bottles were of various shapes with narrow necks and tight-fitting stoppers, and had a tiny spoon with which to take the snuff out of the bottles. Snuff in China was called 'nose smoke', and as the Chinaman had no pockets he carried his snuff-bottle in his capacious sleeves. Sometimes out of his sleeve he would produce a tiny bottle which was plain outside and painted with a miniature design inside. How this was accomplished has often puzzled experts. Various theories have been put forward, the most practical being the use of a tiny brush, small enough to have entered the neck of

Eighteenth century snuff-bottles of Imperial porcelain. In centre, solid piece of mother-of-pearl carved in high relief with cock. Heights: $3\frac{3}{8}$, $3\frac{1}{2}$, 3 ins.

the bottle. No doubt the craftsmen had their own secrets, as had those English craftsmen who managed, another puzzle, to get models of ships into glass bottles.

These designs seem very fancy-free, as if the artist had thought them out for himself, and delighted in this miniature art for its own sake. There are some examples of them to be seen in the Victoria and Albert Museum, which prove that they are none the less exquisite for being so minute. The designs themselves of humans, animals, birds, fruits, etc., tell us little of the bottles' history. Hildburgh, one of the few authorities on this subject, speculates: 'As often as we hold these little bottles in our hands we wish for some magic power that would let us know their history. What Arabian Nights' tales these bottles might be able to unfold for us!' We can only conjecture. . . . For instance, at Sotheby's, we saw a bottle of black lacquer with mother-of-pearl, lotus pools and cranes, which are one of the commonest symbols of longevity.

Again, there was one with a horse, ridden by a monkey and pursued by a bee. Though the monkey is usually looked upon as a symbol of ugliness and trickery, it was worshipped to some extent by the Buddhists. In *Social Life of the Chinese*, Doolittle tells us that an Emperor of the T'ang dynasty deified the monkey who was supposed to have helped the envoy sent by him to India to obtain the Sacred Books of the Buddhist religion. As a reward, the Emperor gave it the title of 'The Great Sage Equal to Heaven'. The monkey was supposed to keep away goblins or evil spirits, so in this design it is probably protecting the horse, emblem of speed and perseverance. As for the bee it is, as in the West, an emblem of industry and thrift: 'As busy as a bee'.

Another monkey was represented on a milk-white snuff-bottle, seated and holding a peach, which is an emblem of marriage and a symbol of immortality and springtime. As the God of Longevity is often depicted emerging from a peach, could it be that snuff, said to be good for one, was thought to prolong life? Speculation could be endless. . . . But the fun is to try to find these bottles for oneself. As one of the Goncourt brothers writes: 'These things which have been the joy of my life, I do not wish them to be consigned to the cold tomb of a museum; but to be disposed of under the hammer to be in the keeping of some inheritor of my own taste.'

One help to the collector is that these bottles are very difficult to imitate.

'It is so lovely, it looks so tiny,' writes an American collector, Lilla S. Perry. 'It is so alone. If you feel this, you are lost, and a new collector is made.'

CHINA AND JAPAN

Chinese and Japanese Lacquer

A gift from the trees

The precious lacquer that we admire on cabinets and screens came from a white sap obtained from the tree rhusvermiciferus in Central and South China. The art of preparing and applying this lacquer is of ancient origin. A human figure in wood with painted lacquer decoration dates as far back as the third century B.C., and is an early example of a tomb figure. One of the first uses to which lacquer was put was to make the earliest Chinese books. For this purpose the hardened lacquer was tied together. By the time of the Han dynasty (206 B.C.–A.D. 220) lacquer had become a popular luxury industry in Szechwan, in the west of China. Already remarkable fantasy showed itself in the designs of birds and animals which were painted in red, usually on a soft dark-brown background. The wooden objects lacquered included toilet sets, pins, combs, cups, trays and even musical instruments.

The Ming dynasty developed the art of carving in lacquer. Coat after coat of the liquid, notable for its rich hue, was applied, sometimes, it is said, even up to two hundred layers, in order to make it thick enough to carve through. As each layer had to be dried before the next was added, the manufacture of the best lacquer work could, in some rare cases, take as much as ten years. Occasionally different colours were used, so that as the carver cut through the layers, he could show the different colours and use them in his designs. These designs were usually of flowers or landscapes, sometimes with figures. Some of the finest examples of carved red lacquer are to be found in the Musée Guimet in Paris, amongst them

Tomato-red lacquer sweetmeat box, in shape of melon.
Diameter: 6 ins. Seventeenth century.

a large red lacquer round box, and an enormous box for holding manu-
scripts. There was also painted lacquer, with symbolic designs.

More intricate still was the inlaid lacquer. When this inlay was of
shells it was called by the Chinese 'misty brocade'. Other inlays were of
jade, turquoise, malachite, rose quartz, lapis lazuli, coral, mother-of-
pearl and ivory. A striking example is a table of black lacquer inlaid with
mother-of-pearl figures, to be seen in the Musée Guimet. But in spite of
this rich and ornamental work, the more simple red Ming lacquer got its
share of praise. In the great Eastern Exhibition of 1936, Frank Davis wrote
in the *Illustrated London News*: 'As an example of refinement of taste, almost
too chaste for Western eyes, they have the harmony of line and colour
which we express rather feebly by using the word *classic*.'

Some of the Ming boldness and vigour were lost, as they were in
porcelain, during the Ch'ing dynasty. Lacquer ware, however, gave full

scope for the detailed and clear-cut designs for which the Ch'ing period is famed. The decorations often consist of intricate formal landscapes with floral designs. The objects range from tiny snuff-bottles and carved boxes to large pieces of furniture, such as the Chair in the Victoria and Albert Museum from the Summer Palace in Peking, and a towering wardrobe of black lacquer, supposed to date from the beginning of the reign of K'ang Hsi, which immediately catches the eye on entering the Chinese room at the Musée Guimet. This is indeed an impressive object. On the front are displayed two dragons, representing longevity, sporting among clouds and waves, while the sides are taken up with intricate inlaid designs of mountains, trees and rocks.

It was perhaps the colours and the carving on the exotic cabinets and screens that first drew the attention of the West, when lacquer was imported to Europe in the seventeenth and eighteenth centuries. This lacquer was greatly admired. A Jesuit Father, Louis Le Compte, who arrived in China in 1687, writes about it: 'For tables and chairs it is sufficient to lay on two or three layers of varnish, which makes it so transparent . . . that it could serve as a mirror.'

A very unusual style of carved lacquer found its way West, under the almost assumed name of '*Coromandel*'. This does not mean, as one would suppose, that it was made on the Indian Coromandel Coast; it was made in fact in China, and exported to the West from that Coast. In this *Coromandel*, usually consisting of large screens, the wood was coated with black lacquer which was afterwards cut away in the shape of floral designs and then very strikingly coloured or gilded. It is a pity that these outsize works of art should sometimes have been cut up to make them fit into the smaller and less majestic rooms of the West, though it is some consolation that one such large screen, split into different pieces, could now delight three or four homes, instead of one.

The art of Chinese lacquering reached its peak under the reign of Ch'ien Lung (1736–95), who was especially fond of carved lacquer. His throne, which can now be seen in Room 44 of the Victoria and Albert

Museum, was made in the Imperial Lacquer Factory. The decoration on it symbolizes good fortune, longevity and marital felicity. The centre panel at the back has an elephant bearing a vase of jewels, meaning 'Peace reigns in the North'. The elephant stands for one of the Seven Treasures of Buddhism, and Buddha himself is supposed to have thrown the elephant, symbol of strength as well as of sagacity and prudence, over a wall. On each side of this throne stands an enormous pair of vases in carved red lacquer, with the motif of the nine dragons pursuing the Sacred Pearls, which also come from the Summer Palace in Peking. We ourselves have seen a very attractive panel of the Ch'ien Lung period, from a cabinet, decorated with a dragon, in a private collection.

The decoration on lacquer often illustrated stories and symbols as well as exploits of warriors. Lacquer was also sometimes used as a sheath for swords, for noble warriors liked to possess a weapon worthy of their prowess on the battlefield.

A spectacular variation on lacquer is the *barjute* (lac-burgauté), with a black background of special lacquer inlaid with mother-of-pearl that shines like opals. A collector showed us the particular shell used for making this mother-of-pearl.

Lacquer, however, had another purpose as well as merely looking decorative. It was used to make ceramics and wood impermeable to water and air, thus helping to preserve food as well as the precious objects themselves. Objects salvaged from shipwrecks, when coated with lacquer, have been found to be unharmed, even after many years. The Japanese proved this also, at the Vienna Exhibition of 1878, when they showed lacquer exhibits undamaged that had been recovered from a shipwreck eighteen months earlier.

No one exactly knows when the Japanese began their own art of lacquering, but there is a Japanese dry lacquer portrait of the priest Ganjin, one of the earliest Buddhist missionaries from China to Japan, that was made soon after his death in A.D. 763 It is also known that in the twelfth century, Japanese lacquer work in the Fujiwara style

Coromandel writing screen with Immort
K'ang Hsi period. 9 by 5

Carved red lacquer box, landscape with figures.
Diameter: 7 ins. Ch'ien Lung period.

imitated some early Chinese lacquer, though showing more vigorous and free decoration. The two great periods of Japanese lacquer were the Monoyama (1578–1615) and the Tokugawa (1615–1868). In their designs the Japanese show themselves to have been more adventurous than the Chinese. Their craftsmen, who were great lovers of nature, were not content with finding a conventional formula and keeping to it. They were always ready to experiment and to try out new designs. Their sense of colour and of the dramatic in nature, combined with their vivid imagination, bewitch the beholder with gaiety as well as beauty.

The Tokugawa period developed the ideas sown in that of the Monoyama, aiming at making their designs even more decorative and original. Prodigal with colour the craftsmen used their imagination to give a jewel-like effect to a design that imitated the pictorial.

Designs often included the famous Japanese mountain Fujiyama, and scenery of lake and river with various fish and animals, fruits and flowers. The tiger is sometimes shown with bamboos in a storm that is obviously going to destroy it, although the bamboo itself will survive, because it bends with the storm.

Objects in lacquer were almost innumerable, large and small, including shrines, wine-cups, toilet-articles, saddles, cabinets, chests (a collector showed us an early nineteenth century chest, profusely decorated and obviously made for export), writing-tables and their accessories, screens, bird-cages, lanterns, trays and boxes. Lacquer tables about a foot high were used at meals, with tiny lacquer and porcelain cups and bowls, dishes and teapots. Shoes made of lacquer were sometimes work by Court ladies, and lacquered wooden pillows were often given as a wedding present.

The Samurai warriors had swords in red lacquer scabbards. A good sword was highly esteemed and a Samurai would go with poor food and clothing rather than be without one to do him honour as a gentleman and a soldier. The proverb on the blade said: 'The girded sword is the soul of the Samurai.'

There were even special boxes for sending letters by messenger. These were bound in silken cords with knots usually shaped as butterflies, and were so precious that the messenger had to wear a cloth over his mouth so that he should not breathe upon the box. There were also boxes for a poem card game. Another game was played with lacquer incense-burners by Japanese nobles and prominent men. The game consisted in guessing the name of the perfume which was being burnt, and there were forfeits for guessing the wrong one. Such pretty trifles strike a rather pathetic note in the Musée Guimet as one looks down through a glass cabinet at the little collection of Marie Antoinette, containing, amongst other objects, a black lacquer box for holding tea and a black writing-box, decorated with gold.

A small lacquer incense-box brought out the innate courtesy of the

Japanese Fan, gold lacquer on tortoiseshell. Circa 1800.

Japanese. It was considered good manners on the part of guests to ask their host if they could examine such boxes, because they had been collected in most unusual shapes such as flowers, butterflies, boats and ducks. Lacquer incense-boxes and burners were also used in the impressive Japanese social function of the 'Tea-Ceremony', although the teapots themselves were usually made of simple earthenware, because they were the symbol of austerity and humility, encouraged by the Buddhist religion. In the fourteenth century the Zen monks had brought from China precious paintings of the Sung period, and while drinking tea they used to contemplate these landscapes of dreams that expressed their philosophy far more clearly than they could express it in words. This custom developed into the famous 'Tea-Ceremony' around the end of the fifteenth century. All objects, including the lacquer tea-bowls, used in this ceremony were required to be beautiful, yet as simple and unostentatious as the conversation of those taking part. The ceremony usually took place in an annex to the main house. In the winter the garden was strewn with fir leaves and the guests kept their shoes on, but in the summer the garden was gay with flowers and the guests took their shoes off. The rules forbade any conversation on politics or scandal. Flattery, also, was not permitted, and the ceremony generally lasted about two hours.

How fortunate were the inhabitants of the East in their lacquer trees, for European Japanned work with its artificial gloss can never achieve the polished surface of genuine lacquer work. The writer Lockyer tells us that some Japanese lacquer he saw was 'of so shining a black that you can see your face in it'. Luckily, a good deal of this lacquer, both Japanese and Chinese, is still to be found today.

Chinese and Japanese Cloisonné

A coloured jigsaw

The word '*cloison*' means cells or partitions, and the metal wires which, in this technique, prevented one colour from running into the other, gave full scope for the skilful putting together of colours in which both the Chinese and Japanese delighted.

Different coloured enamels were mixed in separate containers and then filled into the cells by means of a writing-brush, the result often being a mosaic-like pattern, or a recurring pattern of flowers on the vases, boxes, cups, bowls and above all, sacrificial vessels, treated with this technique. It was soon found that the wares soldered onto the surface of these objects could be bent to any shape and so serve not only to prevent the different colours from fusing together, but also to emphasize the design and give it greater variety.

Some authorities assume that the art of *cloisonné* enamelware was introduced into China in the Yuan dynasty by the Arabs. But looking further back, we find the Chinese using the same technique to apply the designs in different coloured enamels to their pottery as early as the T'ang period, separating the one colour from the other by means of strips of clay. There was certainly interchange in the T'ang dynasty between China and Byzantium, through groups of Arabs who settled in Canton in the eighth century. However, it was not until the Ming dynasty that the art of *cloisonné* really came into its own. The earliest known pieces had a cast bronze base, and very fine wires shaped and placed with great skill. The designs, often of lotus and fungus scrolls and borders of clouds, were simple and clear-cut.

Chinese cloisonné Vase in shape of pilgrim-bottle. Various colours on turquoise ground, decorated with lotus scrolls and dragons. Height: $7\frac{1}{2}$ ins. Sixteenth century.

Chinese cloisonné Vase of square section, decorated with four-season flowers:
lotus, peony, camelia and chrysanthemum; with grape-vine of
typically early Ming (first half of sixteenth century). Height: 8½ ins.

Small cloisonné cosmetic box, peach-shaped. Royal blue ground, decorated with good-luck symbols: bat among lotus-scrolls. $3\frac{1}{2}$ by $1\frac{1}{2}$ ins. Late eighteenth century.

The enamels with their vivid colouring must have appealed strongly to a dynasty that worshipped colour and knew how to employ it to the best advantage on metalwork. The Emperor Ch'ing T'ai (1450–56) took *cloisonné* under his patronage, feeling it to be specially appropriate to the decoration of Temple vessels. Ming *cloisonné* designs are, like all those of the Ming period, bold and vigorous, the principal enamels used generally being turquoise blue, lapis-lazuli blue, dull red, yellow, white and dark green, gilded after the completion of the enamelwork. It is worth noting that in the Ming period the wires are usually of bronze, whereas in the Ch'ing dynasty a change to copper was made.

In the Ch'ing dynasty, the Emperor K'ang Hsi thought highly enough of *cloisonné* to set up a work-shop in Peking for its manufacture. Later, Ch'ien Lung (1736–95) carried on the tradition. Though the colouring itself was sometimes less vivid (the Ming enamels seem to glow more brightly) the colour scheme was more complicated and more gilding was used. One particular design shows an unusual treatment of the dragon's mane which is divided and spreads on either side of the head;

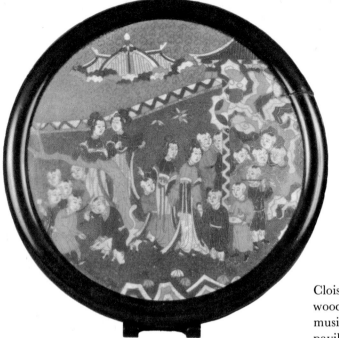

Cloisonné enamel circular plaque, with
wood frame, decorated with ladies,
musicians and other figures in a
pavilion. Diameter: 11 ins. Late Ming.

sometimes one part of the mane is flowing downwards and the other
upwards. A great many examples of *cloisonné*, which can be seen in the
Victoria and Albert Museum, belong to the Ch'ien Lung period. In this
Museum, too, we find a good example of early twentieth century (1904)
cloisonné. On gilt copper, enamelled in *cloisonné*, is a dish on a stand which
is in the form of a winged fish-dragon. This was made for presentation
to Professor Nicholas Orloff and is inscribed: 'His ethical learning is as
the depths of the sea'.

Cloisonné being extremely decorative was sometimes used with other
media. In a screen placed before writers to inspire them in their work,
belonging to a private collection, we find *cloisonné* and jade decorating a
painting of the 'Hare and the Moon'. This is an old Chinese symbol.
C. A. S. Williams, in *Outlines of Chinese Symbolism and Art Motives*, tells us
that it was believed that the moon, representing the essence of the female
in nature, was inhabited by a hare, said to be occupied in pounding the
drugs of immortality at the foot of a cassia tree. The hare itself is an

Hare and Moon Screen, in cloisonné and jade.

emblem of longevity and is often depicted on porcelain. Mayers, in his *Chinese Reader's Manual*, writes that it is 'reported as deriving its origin from the vital essence of the Moon, to the influence of which luminary it is consequently subject. . . . According to a Buddhist legend, the hare offered its body as a willing sacrifice, lying on a pile of dry grass, and was rewarded for its devotion by transmigration to the Moon.'

Because of its rather exotic associations to do with Temple Worship, and its strange, mosaic-like designs, *cloisonné* has not found its way much into modern homes, but recently the discriminating buyer has found that *cloisonné* on vases, bowls, ash-trays, etc., goes well with the gay decorations of the room of today. There are, of course, modern imitations of Eastern *cloisonné*, but the older pieces can be recognized by their softer colours and occasionally more skilful designs. When examining a possibly older piece, supposed to belong to the Ming or Ch'ing period, beware if it has plain enamel inside. A pattern inside, or just metal plain or gilded may be a surer test of its genuine quality.

Interior of Chinese cloisonné shallow bowl, decorated with leaping carps. Diameter: 5½ ins. Late sixteenth century.

Small cloisonné vase in shape of pomegranate. Turquoise ground
with lotus scrolls. Height: 5 ins. Late Ming.

Once the eye has grown used to the technique and the colouring,
through looking, say, at examples in the Victoria and Albert Museum,
it is not difficult to pick up samples of the Ch'ing period.

The technique of *cloisonné* seems to have reached Japan later than
China, in the second half of the eighteenth century. The Japanese often
decorated their swords with *cloisonné*, proof that it was highly thought of

in Japan. Sometimes the bright turquoises and brilliant reds to be found on Chinese *cloisonné* are not so frequent in the Japanese decoration, where softer colours, such as dark green and brown often predominate, quite frequently on a silver base. Very popular were the tiny Japanese water-bottles, made in the eighteenth century.

Towards the end of the nineteenth century a new school of *cloisonné* began in Japan. The Japanese imagination and love of nature led its artists to reproduce the landscapes, flowers, plants and birds which their people admired so much. In 1910, the Japanese Government issued an album of T'ang art. In this could be seen Chinese mirrors decorated on the back with floral designs in what would appear to be *cloisonné* – an apt analogy, showing perhaps that the Japanese, as so often in their art, mirrored the Chinese, but took the skills and made them their own.

JAPAN

Korean Influence on
Japanese Ceramics

Imitation is the sincerest form of flattery

If we were to take, say, three bowls of *blue and white* pottery or porcelain, Chinese, Japanese and Korean, in the seventeenth and eighteenth centuries, we would see that the Japanese and Korean bowls are much more akin to each other than they are to the Chinese. Both Japanese and Korean bowls have simple designs of birds and flowers, sparse and poetically spaced. 'The Japanese,' writes W. B. Honey, 'have always admitted their indebtedness to Korean culture' and although, at first, both countries copied the Chinese models, they soon broke away and developed unique styles of their own. Korea led the way, for already in the Han dynasty (206 B.C.–A.D. 220) China had established its colonies in the country nearest to it, which happened to be Korea. As Korean territory reaches out from Manchuria towards the islands of Japan, several Korean craftsmen went to work in Japan. They had a good incentive for doing this, for in Japan sculptors, potters and metal workers had a social status that they never enjoyed in China, and the greater independence to which this led allowed these immigrant craftsmen full scope for imaginative and varied work. But the immigration of Koreans into Japan was further enforced by the Japanese invasion of Korea in 1592 and again in 1597–98, when Hideyoshi, the conquering general, took some of the potters back to Japan to aid its ceramic industry in the South Island of Kyushu. Later, these potters were to have a strong influence on the development of Japanese Tea-Ceremony wares.

As far back as the Koryo dynasty (918–1392) Korea had won renown for its pottery and porcelain. Even the Chinese had been impressed by

121

the Korean 'Kingfisher Colour'. Korean *celadons* were also very fine and noted for their green or bluish-green glaze, which closely imitated the Chinese but showed originality in their shapes, amongst others, those of gourds and melons. At the beginning of the Yi dynasty in 1392, these fine *celadons* became rougher and more rustic, but these imperfections were outweighed by the lively designs and the strength shown in the brushwork. 'The peasants,' as Gompertz remarked, 'worked with complete freedom to express their own concept of beauty.'

These wares and others did much to influence Japanese pottery after their invasion of Korea in 1592. The spirit of Korean art brought out the sense of design and decoration which was innate in the Japanese. The Japanese religion of Shintoism, which is, to put it simply, gratitude to the beauty and fruitfulness of a benevolent Nature, made their decorators respond to the 'wild, free beauty' that Gompertz speaks of in Korean art. Thus the Japanese tradition of decoration owes more to Korea than it does to China, and any study of Japanese ceramics is therefore greatly enriched by some knowledge of Korean art.

Satsuma

Jewelled ware

Japanese pottery, of which Satsuma is one of the styles best known in the West, often eludes us as to its dates. According to legend, a potter named Kato Shirozaemon came from China early in the thirteenth century and taught the Japanese how to make pottery of a brown glazed type. From about 1227 onwards this pottery was made at Seto, which thus became the classical pottery centre of Japan. These Seto productions typified the stonewares of the early period of Japanese ceramic arts, and lasted until the rules of the Tea-Ceremony had been worked out, according to W. B. Honey, around the end of the fifteenth century. This ceremony, which demanded a high social etiquette, also required more delicate pottery for its perfect fulfilment. The ceremony was, as we have seen, originally introduced by Buddhism, and Japanese pottery itself owes much to this religion. Satsuma played its part in this ceremony, around the end of the sixteenth century. The early specimens are mostly in blue with a little brown, and there are some admirable wares inspired by the Koreans and also some close copies of T'ang pottery, but there are others less pleasing. A Japanese critic gives us a picture of some wares: 'The cracks produced in the firing are in perfect keeping with the powerful modelling and suggestive of the works of nature'; and again: 'The flow of glaze reminds us of moss growing on a stone.'

The sixteenth century had been a period of war and turbulence, but the seventeenth saw the country at peace under strong rule, and as usual, the arts profited. Even the most famous Japanese painters and decorators began to turn their talents to pottery; and to the joy of the

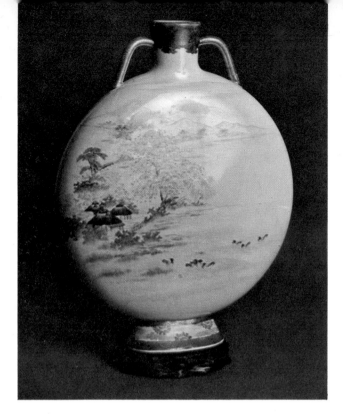

Moon-flask Vase with blossom and ducks.
Height: 12 ins. Nineteenth century.

potters themselves, one of the princes who lived about the middle of this
century used to stamp the best pieces of Satsuma with his seal, before
they were fired. By this time the Satsuma potters had learnt from the
porcelain painters at Arita to use the bright colours, reds, gold, yellows,
greens and silver which we are accustomed to associate with this
enamelled 'jewelled ware'.

Like all Japanese pottery the finest Satsuma shows a sensitive response
to nature as well as to art. The pottery in general is remarkable for the
potter's skill of hand and for the decorator's sense of balance between
background and design. The Japanese were artists even in the arrangement of flowers. Instead of gathering a great bunch they would be content, say, with one sweetly scented branch of cherry or plum blossom
which they would place carefully in a vase that set off its full beauty.
Their rather romantic imagination was fired by the blossom of the

Satsuma vase with cream glaze finely speckled with b
enamelled with a wild goose and young, flying before the full m
Height: 15½ ins. Nineteenth cen

cherry tree. They said that 'cherries whiten the wayside with snow-showers that do not descend from the skies'. This imagination also made them rich in symbolism. D. C. Angus in *The Eastern Wonderland (Japan)* tells us of the 'Feast of Flags', when a hollow paper fish in the shape of a carp about six feet long was hung to a pole. As the wind rose it filled with air and its tail and fins flapped, as if it wanted to swim. The carp, which swims against the stream, symbolized the difficulties boys would have to encounter and the determination they would have to show to overcome them.

An imagination so vivid was surely inherited from the potters of the seventeenth century who certainly expressed their imagination through their designs. Rich in coloured enamels were the Satsuma processions of religious and legendary figures, each figure having its own symbolic significance. One of these was a monk with a hempen bag of Buddhist lore, who was supposed to be going to reappear as the Buddha of the Second Coming and to be styled the Buddhist Messiah. He had a shaven head, a broad, smiling face, large pendulous ear-lobes and was seated beside a capacious bag with a jewel of the law in his hand. His robes were richly embroidered with gold brocade, emblazoned with symbols of precious gifts to bestow upon his votaries. These figures stood out the more strikingly for the glaze being crackled, so that the reflection of the light on it was split up when seen from various angles.

In the finest Satsuma the decorations were not overcrowded and the designs were thoughtfully balanced. As Brinkly wrote about it in the Paris Exhibition of 1867: 'In this field thus newly opened to Western collectors the first place has, by common consent, been assigned to the *faience* (earthenware) of Satsuma. In its combined softness and richness it has no peer.'

In the second half of the eighteenth century, fine Satsuma ware continued to be made at the Tadeno factory in Kagoshima, but by the nineteenth century it tended to become gaudy, with extravagant gilding and crowded designs. This more showy Satsuma, made to suit nineteenth

Satsuma Jar with Buddha Lion.
Height: 31 ins. Diameter: 47 ins.
Late nineteenth century.

Satsuma Vase with figures.
Height: 5 ins. Late nineteenth century.

century European taste, was an unfortunate development of the earlier,
finer style, but nevertheless it found its admirers. An authority, William
Leonard Schwarz, so loved Satsuma that he felt he must break into verse
about it.

> Hence the grace divine,
> Of tracery enamelled on your gown. . . .

In Paris, towards the latter part of the nineteenth century, smart
Japanese boutiques were opened, and one of the Brothers Goncourt
recalls how he used to gaze at his Satsuma, pondering on the attraction
which animals had for the oriental mind. He seems also to have been
fascinated by the type of Japanese woman who occasionally appears on
Satsuma, with her gigantic head-dress, air of modesty and, according
to him, look of hilarious innocence in her eye. We ourselves have seen

such a woman portrayed on the inside of an attractive shallow bowl. With her jet-black hair and rich red dress, decorated in gold, she makes an inviting splash of colour in any room. She is, however, only one of the many nineteenth century Satsuma wares which can be found today, such as cups, tea-jars, incense-burners, plates, vases and small ornaments for the writing-table, decorated with birds, branches and landscapes, brilliant flowers and scarlet cherry blossom, which lend themselves well to the brocaded costumes of the figures that are often portrayed with them. In *Oriental Antiques*, the proprietor and collector, Mr George Horan, showed us a delightful pair of medium sized vases, with the Satsuma white glaze that looks like ivory, completely undecorated except for flowering wisteria drooping over the neck, and a set consisting of two vases and a pot, decorated with brightly coloured flowers. These are very fine examples of Satsuma, but recently we saw more modest wares including a delightful little teapot, and a small and very decorative vase with figures and blossom at Camden Passage (Islington). Imagine this vase magnified almost ten times, so that it stands about four feet high and, decorative though it is, seems rather overwhelming for the average room. Such vases do exist, and find their place happily in a garden, as flower containers, where this 'jewelled ware' competes for first place with the gaiety around it.

Imari or Arita

The street of the coloured decorators

> Through the clear realms of azure drift
> And on the hillside I can see
> The villages of Imari. . . .

Thus wrote the poet, Peter Osbeck, and one can imagine him sailing along the Japanese coast, towards the Port of Imari, from where the Japanese porcelain of that name was shipped to Europe. This porcelain would have come from the town of Arita, straight from 'the Street of the Coloured Decorators', where it was made. Never was a street more appropriately named, for the Arita or Imari porcelains (they are known by both names) were famed for the brilliancy of their colours. These were mostly blue underglaze and overglaze red and gold, the enamelling giving a jewelled effect – quite distinct from the Chinese decorations from which it was originally copied. For, as we have seen, the art of porcelain-making developed in Japan later than in China, and it was only towards the middle of the seventeenth century that the Japanese, with the help of Korean potters, began to copy the Ming and the Ch'ing that they had imported from China.

Exports to Europe began almost at the time when the Dutch took over the Portuguese factory at Nagasaki. This factory had been set up by the Portuguese in 1542, when one of their ships bound for China was driven by a storm into what was for them an unknown land. But in 1639 the Portuguese fell out with the Japanese Emperor, who could think of no ruder way of treating them than by issuing an edict stating that 'the whole race of Portuguese, with their mothers and nurses shall be

Large Arita Porcelain Vase with Phoenix.
Height: 16 ins. Seventeenth century.

banished.' Needless to say the Portuguese had neither mothers nor nurses with them.

These colourful porcelains, originally shipped by the Dutch in large quantities to the rest of Europe, were so much admired that the great European factories, including Delft, Meissen, Chantilly, Bow and Derby, copied them in the eighteenth century when porcelain in Europe really came into its own.

There were two distinct styles of Arita or Imari porcelain. The first, the sparsely decorated Kakiemons, which are mostly museum pieces, and the second, the profusely coloured and decorative Aritas of which there are innumerable specimens to be found in our junk-shops and street-markets today.

The name '*Kakiemon*' derives from a famous pottery family. The first Kakiemon that we know of arrived at Arita in 1615 and worked to produce red overglaze enamels, similar to the Ming which Japan had imported, although his designs soon began to take on an unmistakable Japanese air. Some hold that the name '*Kakiemon*' derives from this red overglaze which was the hallmark of his school, the colour being compared to that of a ripe persimmon or 'kaki'. He was succeeded by other members of his family; for several generations they made quite a clan together. This Kakiemon family succeeded in producing such a perfect white glaze that even the Chinese admired it. It was essentially a glaze that called for sparse decoration, although every delicate touch in the design played its part. The designs included wild roses, which almost came to be a trademark, and other flowers, butterflies and birds, amongst them the quail, in red, yellow, green and blue. Chinese bird and flower themes are spaced out in order to give the peculiar Japanese look. Human figures are rare, but there are many designs of trees. About these, Mr Winthrop, a collector and admirer of old Japanese ware, writes: 'Upon my vase there is what is intended for the "sacred bird" rather than a peacock seated upon a tree, on each panel, the tree in two cases being the prunus, in two a pine, and in two a bamboo. . . .' The prunus, or plum tree, and the pine, or fir tree, were used as symbols at Japanese weddings. D. C. Angus, in *The Eastern Wonderland (Japan)*, tells us that on the table in the bridegroom's house there were images of a fir tree, a blossoming plum tree and a stork standing on a tortoise; the fir tree signifying the strength of the bridegroom, the plum tree, the beauty of the bride, and the stork, the long life desired for both.

The delicate decorations of the Kakiemons make a strong contrast to the second type of Arita. These Japanese decorators began early to produce designs and colouring which were much to Japanese taste. The colourists often depart as far as possible from nature. There is flowing red water, exotic-looking green flowers and blue trees bearing indigo blossom, in fact, colour for colour's sake. It is no wonder that the Japanese have such clear reds on their porcelain, for a dirty-red was supposed to be a sign of ill-omen. The designs are very striking. Some Imari work, easy to find nowadays, looks as if the potters had copied materials used for clothing – lavish designs, looking rather like brocade, often cover the whole surface of a jar or a vase. In addition to these there is the 'hanakagode' or flower-basket pattern. This is the pattern of a wicker-basket, usually with a high loop handle, supporting a profusion of flowers, some of which can be seen through the woven sides of the basket. Pomegranates, as an emblem of posterity, were sometimes depicted:

> The pomegranate gleams with fiery light,
> The pear shines bright and pure, a frosty white.

The pear was a symbol of purity and justice. Another favourite pattern was the formalized chrysanthemum, the 'kiku', which depicts a conventionalized flower-head of sixteen petals within a circle. This pattern caused Jacquemart, the great French nineteenth century authority on the Far East, to crack a joke. Instead of the Chinese *famille rose*, he called the Aritas 'famille chrysanthée'. The Japanese did, in fact, copy the famous *familles verte* and *rose*, although the *rose* was not copied until the nineteenth century.

Designs of animals include the five fabulous beasts: the dragon, the Japanese unicorn, the Buddhist lion, the water-tortoise with the long hairy tail, and the ho-ho bird (the phoenix). Among the animal figures are to be found brown and white piebald dogs with red collars, fish with figures riding on their backs, foxes and reclining stags.

There are not many figures of humans, though sometimes the gods are portrayed. A favourite is one representing longevity, with his grotesquely elongated head and long beard; but there is also the god of Daily Bread, depicted as a fisherman with a large fish attached to his rod. A curious contrast is made between the god of Riches and the god of Contentment. The god of Riches carries a rice-bale and is attended by rats (could this be a premonition of the rat-race?), while the god of Contentment has a bag containing gifts and a troupe of children around him.

Apart from these two famous styles, Kakiemon and Arita, there was a cheaper type of Imari in *blue and white* underglaze, that was almost peasant ware. This ware was called 'Kurawanka', meaning, '*Won't you eat?*' or '*Come and get it!*' The name is appropriate, because when small cargo boats left the Yodo River, food-sellers would anchor off the river bank and would toss bean-paste and other simple fare in cheap dishes of this *blue and white* to the boatmen, who would then hand them to their passengers. Thus the bottom of the Yodo River became littered with broken dishes, the result either of poor throwing or poor catching. Not all of it was broken, however, for this *blue and white* is obtainable in junk-shops and markets in fair supply, slightly cheaper than the coloured wares.

These coloured wares included small bottles, phials, tea-cups, pepper-and-salt boxes, flasks, small mugs, square butter-pots, flower-pots, beer mugs and medicine flasks. There were also innumerable vases. Some of these, in the nineteenth century, are as much as five or six feet tall, and though owing to their size they have become the white elephants of the sale-room, they are often sold at knock-down prices and are good bar-

Pair of Arita Vases, blue and red. Height: 12 ins. Late eighteenth century.

gains for anyone able to give them house-room. Other objects to be looked out for today are vases and bowls of all sizes, toilet-suites, tea-cups, plates and covered jars.

Arita found its way to all parts of the world in the later half of the seventeenth century, but some of its Eastern customers do not seem to have been overpolite about the packing of the wares. There are many complaints about slipshod packing. For example, in 1662, the order for two thousand gallipots destined for an apothecary's shop in Batavia, is said to have arrived incomplete. In 1672 the Princess of Tong-King complained that her flasks had been lost at sea, and in 1674 the Shah of Persia lamented that his salt-cellars and ginger-jars had been imperfectly packed.

In spite of these little mishaps, however, the tremendous export trade remained steady until the popularity of the neo-classical style at the end of the eighteenth century put Japanese wares out of fashion. For almost a hundred years there was little interest in Japanese objects, until in 1864 Commodore Perry opened up Japan and her art began once more to attract the attention of the West. The mania which resulted came to be known as 'Japonaiserie'. Whistler, Monet, Degas, and Van Gogh all fell under its spell, and Toulouse-Lautrec actually dressed up as a Samurai. The writer Bowes went one better: he claimed that the Japanese had invented porcelain! Parisians opened Japanese boutiques, and Tokyo sent collections to Paris, where the shining black lacquer cabinets set off the brilliant red and gold bowls of Imari.

This 'Japonaiserie' craze, unfortunately drew to a close during the first half of the twentieth century, when it was eclipsed by a fresh interest in Chinese objects. Now, however, a new interest has awakened in this 'wild and uncalculable poetry', as W. B. Honey describes Japanese porcelain.

> All the bright flowers that fill the land,
> Ripple of waves on rock or sand,
> The snow on Fujiyama's cone
> The midnight heaven so thickly sown
> With constellations of bright stars,
> The leaves that rustle, the reeds that make
> A whisper by each stream and lake,
> The saffron dawn, the sunset red,
> Are painted on these lovely jars. . . .
>
> PETER OSBECK

Kutani

The nine valleys

There is a Japanese dealer's saying: 'Buy Arita, sell Kutani.' What the dealers actually mean by this is that practically no one, not even an expert, can be quite sure whether a certain piece is Arita or Kutani, but that if it turns out to be old Kutani it is more valuable than a piece of Arita of the same period.

Although authorities differ, it seems that the making of old Kutani, sometimes known as Ko-Kutani, began about the middle of the seventeenth century. Kutani porcelain was heavier and coarser than that of Arita. W. B. Honey goes so far as to compare it to stoneware, but perhaps this very solidity was in keeping with the vigour and power of the decoration. All the authorities are unanimous in praising Kutani's beauty of colour, its free and imaginative brushwork and its poetic use of balance and space in the design. It is held by some to be the most characteristically Japanese of all the porcelains produced in the Islands of Japan and, when at its best, it is certainly one of the most exciting. Perhaps this is why the word 'fuku', meaning happiness, is very often to be found as a mark on the old Kutani ware, as well as the 'Kutani' or 'nine valleys' words themselves, for its wonderful decoration certainly gives happiness to the beholder.

The triumph of Kutani lies in its enamels which are always rich and harmonious, whether they be transparent and brilliant or subdued and opaque. The predominant enamel on old Kutani ware was green. Sometimes the whole piece was covered with a deep-green glaze, making the perfect background for the forceful and simple designs of fruit, flowers, fans, etc., which were usually in black, purple and yellow. This vivid green was the great glory of the Kutani decorators, who used their colours just as freely and freshly as if these had indeed been ordinary painting colours. The green has often been thought even more magnificent than the Chinese *famille verte*, of which it was the contemporary. Perhaps the religion of Shintoism, a thankfulness and awe for the wonder of nature, helped to inspire this green for, as a Japanese poet expressed it: 'Manifesting itself is the awe-evoking Deity, even in a single leaf or the weakest grass-blade.'

Besides this 'green Kutani' as it was called, other styles of the older Kutani had decorations of a peculiarly dull red, almost brownish, comparable to the Ming red of the Chia-Ching period (1522–66) slightly tinged with gold. This style was imitated in the nineteenth century, but the gilded decorations in red and gold with their crowded designs are very much inferior to the older pieces.

Another brilliant colour was a blue, almost of the intensity of Prussian blue, used with green, yellow and a manganese purple, rather like the Chinese aubergine. At Polesden Lacey in Surrey can be seen an amusing butterfly-cage, given by the late Queen Mary to her friend, Mrs Ronnie Greville, decorated in green, red, white and this same aubergine, in open lattice work.

It must not be assumed that all nineteenth century Kutani lacks wonder. In *Oriental Antiques* we saw an enormous and very fine bowl, decorated on the outside with a chrysanthemum and leaf pattern of aubergine and blue, yellow and green. Inside, the decoration is divided into three panels, one with a peacock and pink peonies and the other two with landscapes with figures, varying slightly from each other. The bottom of the bowl has a leaf design that almost repeats the colours of the outside.

The designs on old Kutani plates are of special interest; they include peonies and butterflies, lotuses and herons. These plates are often framed

Jade with Lotus Design. Ch'ien Lung Period.

Wine Vessel. Ch'ien Lung period.

with bold textile and diaper patterns, which have a refreshing spontaneity. Other objects were bottles, made to contain 'saki', the rice-wine of Japan. This wine, warmed, was handed to every guest on his departure in small cups with figures of the gods of good luck at the bottom. Jars, cups, teapots, vegetable dishes and incense-burners were also made, some following the Chinese models of late Ming and early Ch'ing periods, with birds, flowers and landscapes; others more like Arita in design and colour. The Japanese imagination was so fertile that it is rare to find two pieces decorated with the same design.

The search for Kutani is unfortunately seldom rewarded, most of the best pieces having never left Japan, and even nineteenth century copies seem to have somehow eluded export. But one thing is certain. If you are fortunate enough to come across a piece of old Kutani it is possible that you will recognize it, for the decoration is so strong that, in the words of an authority on Japanese ceramics, it 'hits you with a bump'.

Nabeshima

The aristocrat of Japanese porcelain

Going into *Oriental Antiques* recently, our attention was caught by an exquisite plate of a glistening whitish-blue glaze, rather like snow when a certain light falls upon it in the early evening. This plate was decorated in a rather restrained way, so as to show the pure beauty of the glaze, with something that can only be described as a movement of blue looking like waves, and designs of an orange-red and green leading up to the flying horse on clouds which crowned the whole. This 'princely piece', as it may well be called, is a late eighteenth century descendant of the porcelain made for the exclusive use of the noble family of Nabeshima, with the help of Korean potters, at Okasachi, a few miles from Arita. Such porcelain with its peerless glaze was indeed worthy of the noble family from whom it took its name. Some early wares seem to have been made about 1660, when the factories first started, with materials from Arita, but Nabeshima's best known and finest period is probably contemporary with the reign of Yung Cheng in China (1723–35).

So proud was the Prince of Nabeshima of his porcelain that, at first, he would not allow it to be sold, but gave it away to his family and friends, though later it was put on the market. Apart from the quality of the porcelain itself, the painting on the designs was outstanding, for by the end of the eighteenth century the Japanese were to lead the East in this field. Only the best models survived the strict discipline maintained at the kilns and were allowed to be sent out to serve the tables of the wealthy families of Japan.

Nabeshima Plate with flying horse. Diameter: $13\frac{1}{2}$ ins. Late eighteenth century.

The early decoration is mainly in the Kakiemon style, though sometimes it imitates some of the sixteenth century Ming wares. The porcelain of the mature *Nabeshima* is more lustrous than that of Arita, and the red has a more orangey tint. The colours used blend harmoniously together, and very often one motif, such as a winter landscape, or a landscape with waves or trees, was splashed freely over the whole surface of the plate. Sometimes it even fell over the edge and was carried on on the reverse side, as if the painter's enthusiasm for his subject had been so great that he could not bear to leave off. There were many designs of bamboo trees, considered one of the most beautiful trees in Japan and, as in China, an emblem of longevity, because it is an evergreen. As the Japanese were very much influenced by China, it is possible that they associated the bamboo with the Chinese legend of filial piety. C. A. S. Williams tells us that a son had 'a sick mother who longed for bamboo shoots in winter, and he wept so copiously on her account that his tears, like the warm rains of spring, softened the hard wintry ground and caused the tender shoots to burst forth, in reward for his filial affection.'

Nabeshima designs, perhaps from the very boldness of the decoration which requires space, seem to have lent themselves to larger rather than to smaller objects. As well as plates, flower-vases were popular. In *Oriental Antiques* we saw a very fine nineteenth century one, decorated with two fishes and red, blue and turquoise flowers. It had panels in the sides with geometric patterns of balls of pink and turquoise on a dark blue background, glistening with meshes of gold. There was also a *blue and white* bowl, with a large, surrealistic kind of animal on it and a 'comb-formation' in *blue and white,* a speciality of Nabeshima porcelain, running round the base.

This porcelain was so highly rated in Japan that its export was very limited, and it is a fortunate collector who might find a piece of this ware 'fit for Princes', as Nabeshima remains until this day.

Netsuke

Fantasy stretched to its limit

If you are visiting an oriental room in a museum you will very likely come across a glass cabinet inside which are a number of little boxes in lacquer and other materials with the most curious objects, such as one sometimes sees in dreams, attached to them. These little boxes, used for carrying some kind of medicine, are called '*inro*' and were carried from a girdle, such as a sash, or tucked into the waistband, at the opposite end of which was the curious object or '*inetsuke*' which held the *inro* and other objects to the girdle. As we know, the Japanese male dress had no pockets, and the *netsuke*, which derives from the words '*ne*' (a root) and '*tsuke*' (to fasten) was soon used with not only the medicine boxes (*inro*) but tobacco-pouches, purses, drinking-gourds, seals and keys.

But why these fantastic shapes, these unreal creatures? Originally, around the beginning of the seventeenth century, the *netsuke* was simply a piece of wood made to serve its purpose as fastener, but the Japanese imagination soon took hold of it, and a number of carvers eagerly seized the chance to put their skills into the fashioning of this miniature art. The most surrealistic sculpture of today could hardly surpass the objects which these *netsuke* carvers created: ghosts, goblins, fox-women, skulls, masks, grotesque figures in every sort of position, all kinds of queer creatures and animals out of stories from Chinese and Japanese folklore and legends. For instance, the 'Chinnan' who rides across a stream on his hat, or 'Ikkaku', a horned magician with a woman on his back. The shapes were as curious as the subjects, and do not lack a sense of humour. Any substance whatever that would lend itself to intricate carving was used by the ingenious craftsmen. Ivory was a favourite material, especially at the beginning of the nineteenth century, when the objects carved included, besides the more exotic ones, snakes, insects, frogs, rats, hares and shells. The ivory carving of the Japanese is well known for its exquisite detail, which matched the ingenious designs. But the *inro* or other objects carried on the girdle were in themselves things of beauty; and the *netsuke* carvers often used materials to match them, such as mother-of-pearl, amethyst, shagreen, agate and lacquer.

By the middle of the nineteenth century, however, these *netsuke* carvers were in danger of being put out of work. The Japanese began to adopt western dress, so the *netsuke* was no longer needed to hold the *inro* on girdles. Until this time Japan had been more or less isolated from the rest of the world, but now treaty ports were opened, and Americans and Europeans started to trade with Japan.

Luckily for the carvers, the newcomers took a great fancy to the fascinating and unusual little *netsuke*, and ordered large quantities of it for export. So intrigued by these objects were they that they commissioned them simply as ornaments without cord-holes, and larger than the originals. Soon, from about 1879 onwards, *netsuke* objects were being made to suit the tastes of tourists in the form of children with baskets, toys, peasants with cockerels, dolls and puppets.

Netsuke of all kinds can be found today, though the older and more rare objects fetch into the hundreds. Like snuff-bottles, these small *netsuke* objects have a peculiar appeal of their own, and are eagerly sought after by some collectors nowadays.

APPENDIX

Chinoiserie

Distance lends enchantment

And inside – all tea-things
And dragons and bells,
The Show-rooms all show, the sleeping rooms cells,
But the Grand Curiosity's not to be seen:
The Owner himself, the old fat Mandarin.

W. HONE: The Joss and his Folly

Today the Pavilion at Brighton may seem too familiar to most of us to be 'the queerest of all the queer sights I've set sight on', as it was to the writer W. Hone, but it does nevertheless strike an incongruous note amongst the dignified Regency architecture of the town. What are all these minarets and domes doing? ('Huge teapots all drilled round with holes'). Just as surprising inside, what are these strange water-lily chandeliers and paintings of Chinese landscapes in scarlet, gold and yellow lacquer on the walls; this dome-shaped ceiling painted like an immense palm tree, with a silver dragon among the leaves holding in his claws a gigantic chandelier. . . . More dragons, this time gilded ones, holding lotus-shaped lamps; and Worcester porcelain of an oriental design, in blue, scarlet and gold?

Yes, the Mandarin is certainly missing, and with him some of the genuine oriental porcelain of the East. It is true that the East invented in their export porcelain designs which they thought would appeal to the West, but the West also created designs out of their imagination of what they thought the East was like. What we have been looking at may be summed up figuratively by the personal vision of Herold of

Meissen: 'There are bright colours and gold – spidery figures of Chinamen and buildings, either excessively high or very long and low, according to the shape of the vessel on which they are painted.'

This then is *chinoiserie*. Credit or blame for its revival has been given
to the Prince Regent in the early nineteenth century; but the Regent
was only following a very old European tradition which dates back as
far as the time of Marco Polo in the thirteenth century. Our traveller up
the ages would then have seen Chinese silks appearing mysteriously in
European cathedrals. Going on to the mid-fourteenth century in
Germany he would have come across a cope embroidered with a Chinese
fret pattern, and if he had been to Prague, at about the same time, he
would no doubt have been surprised to meet Saint Ursula in a dress
resplendent with chinoiserie phoenixes. He would have seen strange
happenings at the Medici Court – amongs the queerest, perhaps, were
extraordinary caricatures of the porcelain he had learned to love so well
in China. In Holland, shortly afterwards, these caricatures seemed almost
the genuine article, except that the birds, the buildings and the flowers
all look slightly strange. In the Court of Louis XIV, the Sun King, panels
of long-tailed birds, dragon-flies and dragons, were placed in exotic
gardens. And in England in the seventeenth century were found more
queer and exotic designs on the English delft ware. There were curious
plates, too, at Bristol, decorated in blue and white with the figure of a
Chinaman squatting in a rockery. One might have seen a vase with a
design that looked like a mandarin's picnic, but on being examined more
closely turned out to be the story of Lot from the Bible. All this fore-
shadows the jingle by James Cawthorn, written a century later:

> Our farms and seats begin
> To match the boasted villas of Pekin;
> On every hill a spire-crowned temple swells
> Hung round with serpents and a fringe of bells. . . .

Everywhere our traveller goes now, Worcester, Derby, Bow, Meissen, Chantilly, Mennecy, this great craze for copying oriental porcelain is breaking out. This magical Land of the East, so far away, is now to be seen on practically every teacup, not as it really is, but as the West, whose eyes have been lent enchantment by distance, imagines it to be:

> Ching-a-ring-a ring-Ching! Feast of lanterns!
> What a chop of chop-sticks, hongs and gongs,
> Hundred thousand Chinese, crinkum-crankums,
> Hung among the bells and ding-dongs!

But, suddenly, China disappears. No more dragons, no more phoenixes, and instead, Roman urns. On to the nineteenth century and back it comes again, not only in the pavilion at Brighton, but on vast porcelain vases of Mason's ironstone, garishly brilliant, and on Spode's pretty *blue and white* printed tea and dinner services.

Today, our traveller will find chinoiseries and genuine oriental porcelain jostling each other side by side on the shelves. Nor should he despise this so-called *chinoiserie*, for anything created with such a feeling of enchantment has magic in it that time cannot steal:

> Bright birds that eternally flew
> Through the boughs of the may, as they sang,
> 'Tis a tale was undoubtedly true
> In the reign of the Emperor Hwang. . . .

Further Reading

AUDSLEY and BOWES: *The Ceramic Art of Japan*. Liverpool Press, 1875.

BOULAY, ANTHONY DU: *Chinese Porcelain* (Pleasures and Treasures). Weidenfeld and Nicholson, 1963 (London).

BUSHELL, S.W.: *Chu Yen: Description of Chinese Pottery and Porcelain, being a translation of the T'ao Shuo*. Oxford University Press, 1910.

DONNELLY, P.: *Blanc de Chine*. Praeger, 1969 (New York).

GARNER, SIR HARRY: *Oriental Blue and White*. Praeger, 1971 (New York).

GULLAND, W. G.: *Chinese Porcelain* (Vols 1 and 2). Chapman and Hall, 1928 (London).

HART, JUDITH and BURLING, ARTHUR: *Chinese Art*. New York: Bonanzo Books, 1953.

HOBSON, R.L.: *Wares of the Ming Dynasty*. C. E. Tuttle, 1962 (Vermont).

HONEY, W. B.: *Ceramic Art of the Far East*. Macmillan, 1945 (London).

JENYNS, SOAME: *Later Chinese Porcelain*. Faber (London).

—: *Ming Pottery and Porcelain*. Faber, 1963 (London).

JENYNS, SOAME and JOURDAIN, MARGARET: *Chinese Export Art in the 18th Century*. Country Life (Spring Books), 1950 (London).

LLOYD-HYDE, J.: *Chinese Porcelain for the Export Market*. R.E.S. Lisbon.

MEDLEY, MARGARET: *Handbook of Chinese Art: A Guide for Collectors, Curators, and Dealers*. International Publishers Service, 1964 (New York).

PRODAN, MARIO: *An introduction to Chinese Art*. Spring Books, 1966 (London).

SAVAGE, GEORGE: *Porcelain Through the Ages*. Penguin, 1963 (Maryland).

SWANN, PETER: *Art of China, Korea and Japan*. Praeger, 1963 (New York).

WILLIAM, C.A.S.: *Outlines of Chinese Symbolism and Art Motives*. Shanghai: Kelly and Walsh, Ltd., 1932.

WILLIAMSON, G. C.: *The Book of the Famille Rose*. C. E. Tuttle, 1970 (Vermont).

WILLS, GEOFFREY: *Jade*. Arco Publications, 1959.

Index

155